MIKE H. ALE

The Melancholy, of a cosmic poet

First published by Self-published 2023

Copyright © 2023 by Mike h. Ale

All rights reserved. No part of this publication may be reproduced, stored or transmitted in any form or by any means, electronic, mechanical, photocopying, recording, scanning, or otherwise without written permission from the publisher. It is illegal to copy this book, post it to a website, or distribute it by any other means without permission.

This novel is entirely a work of fiction. The names, characters and incidents portrayed in it are the work of the author's imagination. Any resemblance to actual persons, living or dead, events or localities is entirely coincidental.

Mike h. Ale asserts the moral right to be identified as the author of this work.

First edition

ISBN: 978-0-7961-3998-6

Cover art by Simone Angelique Maloney
Cover art by M. S. Maloney

This book was professionally typeset on Reedsy.
Find out more at reedsy.com

To the people I love,
Mom, Dad, little sis, big bro,
And all my cousins and friends.

Always know that I love you guys.

And one more, to the woman I will love someday.

Tarry not long, my love,
Lest I lose my heart to madness in life's foray.

Contents

Foreword

This is a collection of poetry that I have worked on for quite a while, in musings with my own thoughts and existential fears.

But this is the reason I wish to share these works because, to me, the full experience of all emotions is the ultimate form of enlightenment.

I am not a new voice, nor one who has the experience to talk about life. I am a young man looking for that light.

You know the one, the one we all want and search for, but never truly find.

So, if you will, take a trip through my chaotic mind, and though dishevelled, silly, and at times dark and obscene.

I hope that you can feel something, if it's not sadness, then let it be jest. If not jest, may your worries, in my hopeless prose, be put to rest.

And don't forget to put on a smile as your resolve is put to the test. And I will make sure that my poetry is, if nothing else, from the soul.

I also hope that my poetry will be impactful in some way and will give you a chance to question the fickle veil of consciousness that we claim is reality. Separating that which we fear and that which we do not know. Scaring us with stories of the survivors and speaking in tongues.

Beyond this, I must ask that you excuse the romanticism; I tend to be a romantic at heart, and my wishes, though infantile and rather immature to some, are truly from a sullen poet's heart. I suppose I can also say that I endeavoured to have a healthy sense of self-awareness present in my writing.

Truthfully, poetry is a beautiful medium to convey thoughts, emotions, and feelings. Yet the beauty of the medium is held in the ability to convey a moment in time to the reader almost discriminantly and with a healthy understanding of the poet's inherent flaws coupled with the world's cruelty.

And in every poem I write, I hope I will be able to convey the best and worst of my heart poignantly to every reader who happens to stumble upon my rather silly book of prose. Composed by a man who thinks too much and written by a fool who thinks he knows too much.

Perhaps it is the promise of a sullen soul, to love the universe that cruelly shall toss you aside someday. Yet still to write of her beauty and your adoration for her. However, as stated before, I tend to be a hopeless romantic. Due to this, I suppose, I can be considered an untrustworthy witness. However, I would argue that love itself is the only one worthy to touch a judge's gavel.

Perhaps there is little I would be able to promise you as the reader, except for my commitment to pour my heart into every word and prose in this book. A very introspective, and at times lamentable process which many times, rids the heart of answers, yet fills it with ever more questions.

And yet, truthfully, I will always write, whether to share with a world of scars or to simply cherish in a small leather-bound book for the rest of my years on this earth. Perhaps there is much to preface this book, and I would prefer it if you were enjoying the poetry instead of me getting you all caught up here.

So in closing, I'd like to say that this debut collection is chronological in nature and chapter-based. In many ways, it's a stream of consciousness of thought from one poem to the next. Every poem represents to me a snapshot of my thoughts, feelings, ideas, or plans. And I suppose sharing this with the world is strange in its own right. But sharing it with people I know may relate may be one of the biggest reasons for writing this book.

Once more, I'll try to keep this brief. Thank you for purchasing this book; I appreciate every minute that you will allow me to spend with you. In conversations with an old friend next to a crackling fireplace, underneath the lonely stars. Sharing stories and laughing the night away.

-Mike H. Ale

Preface

What is life, but a series of plays, run by a madman,
and loved by a jester?
But oh! Hopeless ones!
Heed my words!
don't forget that always,
And forevermore,
will you peace, in a lover's embrace find!
– The poet who made this book.

The melancholy of the dead

Tears of a child,
  Stain the Satin silk,
  Of a fair maiden.

As her silent smile,
  Fills with a dark shadow,
  As her despair is bathed in hopeful defile.

A woman winces at a touch,
  As her lover lowers his gaze,
  As he begs for not too much.

A mother clings to her child,
  With the claws of a wasp,

Hoping never to let go,
  Hoping never to feel lost.

But no end to love do I see,
  Only pain, misery and melancholy.

As the spirits churn and the shadows dance,
  As the beings call for a sacrificial lamb.

Who next to the slaughter?
  Who next to be burnt?
  As the night fills with laughter,

As ash, from flesh,
  Can you no longer discern.

Beg for an end,
  Hope for someone,
  Your wounds to attend.

For with a bony tap of their claws,
  Which echoes through the night,
  Do the dead ones, hope to cause more than fright.

Run,

Don't even think,

Don't even consider,
  The possibility of imagination.

Or plays on the mind,

Or a trick of the light,
  Which pierces the foggy night.

Heed my words,

Lest you trust your own heart,

Run from them all, lest you hope from love to part.
Pain shall follow,

She shall bear her claws,

But run, I ask.

Run, I beg,

Run,

Run,

Run, from the melancholy of the dead.

They are beautiful in their own way

Of an end do I dream,
An end to the shadows,
Which the borders of time do glean.

An end to the bony fingers,
And rotting flesh,

The unholy, ungodly tinder.
Which many a soul,
From love, hath rend.

Which many a lover hath unfurl.
Whom many a tear hath spent.

She walks in a stagger,
As her feet light the floor,

Tired, beaten and haggard.
She cries for love forevermore,

He begs for a change,

As his life waxes and wanes,

At the hands of fate, his captors.
Who deliver unspeakable pain.

A child begs for relief,
As a mother's embrace cold to the touch.

As the cold ones, to the imagination,
Don't leave much.

They beg,
They plead,
They cry,

They are in torment.

For what?
No one shall know.

As the shadows,
Deliver their final blow.

But what a foolish tale to spin,
For a man,
Lost in sin.

As shadows, and bony fingers,
Line my room,

As the shadows have called,

For an early doom.

"Love not, oh reader,"
But such a request is unfair to you.

Then "Cry not, oh child",
But a cold touch can be utterly true.

Beg not for love,

Beg not for pain,

For the shadows deliver it all,
And seldom do they do it in vain.

It shall not pass,
It shall never wane,

For the shadow of life,
And the shadow of death,

Are beautiful in their own way.

The warning

Despair that friend of old,
  Who permeates the winter cold.

A frost of which I could never tell,
  As the withered shadows, this land hath befell.

When hope a strange concept filled,
  And death, a mother's spirit tilled.

As children lay the cobblestone bare,
  With bodies of the broken and fair.

As the beckoning of a broken clock,
  As the spirit is beaten with a rock.

So too do I see,
  What evils have befallen me.

And with a blind eye do I cry out,
  As the evils of the world mount.

So too does my shadow cry,
  Not of sadness but of joy.

As the freedom of evil takes hold,
  So too, do the shadows become more bold.

So, lock your door at night, if you please.
  And answer not to wails and pleas.

For once more do the shadows come,
  To steal the future of all who run.

To break the hope of a little one's heart.
  To steal and kill and break apart.

But what more could a sullen poet say?

You wouldn't listen at the end of the day.

The shadows shall consume,
  And engulf in flame.

And too your heart shall lose its way.

So, run.

Run.

Once more I warn.

Run away

The midnight hour

Suddenly do I sit up straight,
As my mind,
Recalls my fate.

Or imagines one,
On my behalf,
While I beg for the morning sun.

The silence deafens my ears,
As the shadows morph,
Into my greatest fears.

Just a cast of the light,
Just a trick of my sight,

No need to worry or fright.
No evil haunts the night.

But woe to the mind,
Whom solace,
In these lies find.

Yes, a great claim,
Do I here make,

Here must I thee warn,
To read more,
Can cause much harm.

For a mistress must ye never tempt,
And the greatest of all,
Fate, must ye never contempt.

For though her beauty fair,
Her bony claws,
Are filled with despair.

Though young and meek,
Her existence,
Must we never seek.

She waits for the ignorant to fall,
So that they too,
Her name shall call.

For her hair though fragrant,
Gaze not into her eyes,
For they are vacant.

Yes, a lover of man is fate,
But so too a despiser of man.

For though I've seen,

The inexplicable,
The terrible and the obscene.

My mind cannot fathom thus,
Her hold over my heart,
And her hold over my dreams.

Every love have I chased,
To the ends of the earth,
Lest they her patience do test.

So, I shall end my speech here,
A horrid tale,

Lest an unfortunate soul be laid to rest.

I write this poem,
In a last act of despair.

As I warn ye all,
Fear the lady fair.
For if you, her lies do wed,

Shall your eternity,
Be filled with despair.

I warn once more,

Fear.......

Fear.......

Fear the lady in red,

The lady who weds,

Fear the lady in red,

For her thirst,

Shall never be fed.

Fear her,
  Be filled with dread.

For those whom her love do take,
  Have been sentenced to death.

The way of misery

What do I see?
  What must I see?

No matter what they say,
  All I see is misery.

Horror and tragedy.
  Slander and adversity.

Shall I pluck my eyes out?
  For a joy, I could live without?

Lest that joy from lies is formed,
  And every mortal,
  Her lies have adorned.

More lies to quell the call?

Madame or monsieur?

More hope shall I pour?

Before you beg for more?

And beg we shall.
  For hope, once more to sell.

To the next unsuspecting buyer,
  To the next Mademoiselle.

And as swift as she came,
  She'll never come back again.

Once the hardships start,
  Once the dead ones call their name.

The end beckons us all,
  But for some,
  Ignorance is their final fall.

Let the hopeful ones hope,
  And let the free ones be free.
  But as for me,

Well,

All I really see,

Is misery

To cry as a child

The shining gates have opened,
   The floor filled with gold.

As Angels sing their immortal songs,
   As, before me,
   Do I see friends, new and old.

As the sick and twisted cells fall,
   From a body filled with death.

And the light burns all that are left.

But suddenly I look and I see,

Nobody singing, no golden streets.

As the wilderness bears its claws,

I run,
   An infantile, stupid man,

I run.

She claws at time, waiting for my soul.
To banish into the nothing.

The nothing which I denied,
For in hopeful mirth, was I so bold.

To believe the lies, for which,
My heart had taken hold

And in a whisper, a blinking of the eye,
Was I gone and erased from all of time.

As the nothing and everything, swallowed me once more.
I was filled with a nostalgic thought of woe.

"To death am I stranger, but to misery.
To her, am I a lover.
For now, and for all eternity."

And with that self-righteous, arrogant thought.
Did I plunge myself in her arms.

As she whispered comforting words in my ear.
The last of which,
I shall ever hope to hear.

"Here my love, I have waited a while.

Now hurt no more, Oh mortal mere"

Said she as I was drawn into her embrace.
  With the smell of sweet perfume,
  And a beautiful, womanly smile.

Our hearts, ever more, interlaced.
  Once more to roam and wither beyond breath,
  Once more in her womanly arms,

To cry as a child.

The shadows of the damned

They shout at each other,
  But nothing is heard.

As the shells of flesh,
  Make their way towards nothing,
  As they move akin to a herd.

To the lights and music afar,
  As the air is filled with treacherous war.

A man falls as they move mindless,
  Towards the safety,
  Of the spineless.

He's trampled as he yells,
  "Don't leave me, for I have fell!"

A woman cradles a blanket wrapped with charms,
  As her child begs at the street corner, for want of alms.

They beg and plea,

For an end to their melancholy.

But it doesn't come,
As the suited ones hold arms outstretched.
As the poor ones reach for a gun.

Not to harm their neighbours' charms.
But to put an end,
To their want of alms.

In all the screaming,
Could nobody hear.
The laughing and jeering,

Of the shadows, far and near.

Who watch in jest as we walk on glass,
To find an end to the unholy mass.

"There is no hope" the crooked ones jeered,
As they pulled a young man into the land of fear.

"There is no love" the lonely ones sneered,
As they pushed a young woman off a pier.

Both man and woman in a pit of despair,
As children lay frightened by the shadows of were-

And I stood baffled and shocked,
As the suited ones had stolen our lot.

With claims of pain and torture from castles and counts,
Who wear their suits as they call for their plot.

I laughed a terrible laugh,
As the hopelessness sunk in.

As the shadows showed the damned no remorse,
For they had forgotten their kin.

But none of it mattered as the final trumpet blew,
And the light had called for land anew.

In the ashes of old,
The poor ones perished,
As the suited ones held hands in the holes they cherished.

And once more I laughed a terrible laugh,

As the land was once more laid.
With the castles of the counts,
Over the bones of the dead.

But the dead have no voice,

And neither could they stand

As they choose death once more,

To be the shadows of the damned.

The dead man's call

Haven't you heard?
Can you not tell?
Of a darkness, which this land has befell?

A sorrow which that way went,
For which all hope and joy,
Was hitherto rend?

They never screamed,
Or wailed,
Or yelled.

As their souls were taught death,
Their eyes were taught fear,
And their hope was felled.

A prison needed them not,
As with horrid dreams, they plagued,
For which freedom was nary a thought.

"Beg ye children of Adam!

Scream Ye daughters of Eve!

He has come, sinner of sinners!
To take ye all to the land of the eternal eve.

To the land of sorrow and mead,
To the land from which even death shall flee."

Expressionless they walk,
All in a single file,
To the end of the fork.

Millions in the same,
With no dreams,
With eternal shame.

And one final choice they make,
As the abyss stares into their eyes,

And with a light tug of fate,

Take the plunge,

To their demise.

Their brothers and sisters cry not,
Just a hint of joy,
For they have chosen their final lot.

And into death's arms,
Do they, their final choice,

Employ.

I am the man,
Who this poem has authored,
With broken heart.

The man who has chosen,
To play his final part,

In a play of wonderous woe,
As behind the next man,
Am I walking in tow.

To an eternal choice,
For which I have chosen my lot.

To quell the voice,
Who eludes my thoughts,

A vague memory,
Of cherry lipstick and flowers.

For whom the image,
I have searched,
Many an hour.

But nary a being, has there ever been,
Who could my heart so capture.
As the woman in that dream.

Truthfully, not a woman,

Have I ever, hitherto met,

Nor any person who didn't see.
The essence of misery,

For which I was given,
For which, no one has wept.

Cry not for me oh shadows,

Beg not for my life, oh devils,

I go to a better place.

One of toil and strife,

One for which,
I have forsaken my life

One final choice do I there make,
Not as a man,
But one who is damned by fate.

Into the abyss,

I fall,

As with a final breath,

I shall answer to,

The dead man's call.

The forest's curse

I walk through a dark forest,
Filled with a holy chorus.

One of danger and strife,
One which begs to have your life.

For a moment am I struck,
With a bit of rotten luck.

As the ground gives way to sand,
I find water in the place of land.

I swim in vain,
As shock gives way to pain.

As the water and words curl,
As the death of life begins to unfurl.

With one final breath do I regret,
A joy which I always had left.

To a chance or happenstance,
The type you find in an old-fashioned romance.

But now you see,
I was never truly free.

Because the death of life creeped,
And into my life had it slowly seeped.

But now do I die in vain,
As darkness takes the place of pain.

And the cold is lost in time,
As I end my life on a rotten rhyme.

But the end of my tale is this not,
As is the case with my lot.

For awake but sopping am I,
As I search for a reason as to,
Why I didn't die.

I search around but couldn't see,
The beautiful brown eyes staring back at me.

And suddenly did I sit up,
As she pulled me down while making a fuss.

Not a word was exchanged as I realised,
That on her lap was my heart revitalized.

And now she sang a beautiful song,
One which could right all wrongs.

And a holy glow did I see,
As her voice made me feel more than free.

And finally, after a moment of glee,
Did my heart get stung by melancholy.

"Who are you?" I asked,
As she stared down into my heart.

"I know not, I am, isn't that all that matters?" She says,
As her eyes fill me with dread.

"Why am I here?
In this forest of fear?"
I ask, as my eyes start to tear.

"A life for a life says I, and had yours ended,
Surely would I have cried."
Said she as her gentle hand on my forehead did glide.

"Are you the fated one?
She who seeks the sun?"

"The sun, the sun.
Nothing but forest have I from my memory wrung.

What say you of the sun?"
Said she as her face flashed in melancholy.

"For a wish have I been told,
That if I tell you of the sun shall I wonderful riches
Behold." Said I, as my own words did I realise.

"What say you of the sun?
And a wish shall be yours for fun."

"The moon has set and made way,
For the start of a bright new day,
And this frozen heart shall be warned,
By the heat of the charioteer who rides on his way."

When I had finished, did she jump for joy,
As if finally, a vision could she employ.

"Delight! Oh, delight! I have seen the sun through your words,
A wish is yours, my sir, name any number this shall I surely fulfil."

Said she with joy and happiness.

"I wish to show you more,
Of life, of what the earth has in store."

"I wish to show you seas,
Lands far away and lands that freeze."

"My final wish, listen well,
Is for you to be free from this accursed spell."
Did I say as my heart began to swell.

For suddenly was the forest ablaze,
With light and electricity which my mind did amaze.

And suddenly was she free,
As she was suddenly filled with glee.

She ran away and cheered,

As my heart was filled with the pain that I had feared.

Far away shall she run,
Into the world of the sun.

And though she is now free to see,
For this have I unworthy been.

So, I turned to walk,

As my heart had turned to chalk.

And away did I hope to sneak,

As a kiss did I feel on my cheek.
For before me did she stand,
With a suitcase in her hand.

"But why?

Didn't I tell you to see,

That now you are truly free?" Said I in shock.

"Silly, silly. Don't you see,
  That I truly am free,

Free to choose the man with whom I will be,

And one who has seen your melancholy.

Now come and follow me,
  You promised me all that fun,

Who else would I choose but you

To show me the sun?"

The Red String

I beg for a chance,
As the autumn leaves fill my vision,
As they fill it with a glance.

The dark wind blows its song,
And the birds chirp for want of wrong.

And finally, do I find myself in the dark,
With nothing but pain,
To aid my heart.

But a glowing apparition makes itself known,
As the origin of some light was my own.

For on my outstretched hand was a neat bow tied,
Around a red string which to the future did lie.

A red string which further and further went,
As suddenly my heart was caught by what it meant.

I ran faster than I ever have,
And searched for the end of this infernal map.

For at the end would I surely find,
  The reward for the pain that was truly mine.

But silly me, I couldn't see,
  That the further I ran,
  The closer I came to the sea.

The more I followed the red string,
  The more my vision was filled with glee.

For darkness had fallen away and suddenly was my feet,
  Touching the edge of a pier,
  Which kissed the edge of a tumultuous sea.

And a red string which further went,
  Into the water, as far as my heart was rend.

I fell on my knees in want of tears,
  But nothing came,
  As was my fear.

I stared into the abyss,
  As its inviting nature begged,
  In one moment to make me its eternal guest.

And in a moment of weak spirit,
  Did I quickly lurch,
  Toward the end which was for my heart fit.

Deeper and deeper did I sink,
  Before the precipice of the end, I did see.

But suddenly was my arm pulled up,
As the darkness made way,
For a wondrous vision in this accursed sea.

For the string had finally tightened and much to my surprise,
Was I staring into beautiful blue eyes.

And with a silent smile in the deep,
Did we finally meet.

And to realise our last wish,

Did we closer, our hearts bring,

And as we sank,
To the bottom of the sea,

Did we commemorate our journey,
With one act of peace,

One final action did we make,
And with this.
Did we seal our fate,

The darkness engulfed her and me,
And the light did we not miss.
As we welcomed the end,

With true love's,

Final kiss.

And though a short story,
  Ours shall be.

We finally found one another,

At the bottom of the sea.

The dark sun rises

The black sun rises over a misty morn,
  This truth does a sobering dread over me adorn.

Truth be told, had the sun been cheerful,
  Would I still in misery,
  Miss the chance to be happy and peaceful.

For haven't they heard?
  Was the fated tale not spread by a beautiful little bird?

I have died,
  And this is a death for which I harbour no word.

For not a death of my body did I see,
  But a death of the spirit inside of me.

Not a decaying of a physical corpse,
  But the erosion of all that I find in my infernal verse.

No more will my spirit wait for the sun,
  For it will be black anyway,

And the mist is really no fun.

Mourne of the sordid bird's song

I wince and wail,
As the morning rays, over the darkness, does prevail.

A strange light is it today,
As the holy apparitions pierce the mortal day.

A moment of glee,
Before I'm struck once more by melancholy.

Before a sordid bird's song haunts me,
Before the notion of breakfast, instead with dread, does fill me.

Oh, if I could only perceive,
The extent to which my soul does happiness, from me bereave.

But I wouldn't get that far,
If only my back wasn't so strewn with scar.

But still, I shake my head and search,

For a reason to leave my hallowed perch.

I rack my brain in thought,
As the reasons to get out of bed run down to nought.

So, I'm beckoned back to the deep,
As my tired eyes deny the chance of sleep.

And in a silent sigh of defeat,

Do I balance the floor on my feet.

And slowly but surely do I trudge along.

As I listen to that sordid bird's song.

The spirit world calls

The spirit world calls,
An empty shrill which excites and enthrals.

I beg for an escape,
As the shadows flaunt their capes.

As the jesters play their songs,
As I play along.

I live in joy and dread,
As the priests wake the dead.

I hope for a sweet release,
As the shadows pull the last of my peace.

From a corpse, they pull,
The last of all men to rule.

I am the victim of death,
And so are the dead.

For though they have given their last breath,
I have surely died.
This, you surely, will have to accept.

So, alms for this soul,
Come here and fill this bowl!

With coin and jewels,
For my sackcloth to adorn.

You wince at my laugh?
Wish you from my presence to depart?!

Then never glance at this place,
And from the veil, must you hide your face.

Walk into this world at your own peril,
For this land is filled with nothing but devils.

So, hide yourself and run to the hills,
And stay away from excitement and shrills.

Close your ears and beg for shame,

As the call of the spirit world.

Is all but tame.

The fall

I break a leg on my ambition,
  Hoping for the intended reward to come to fruition.

I wait for the universe for once, to play fair.
  But in the end am I choked of the last of my air.

A messy friendship do I form,
  As I, another man's soul adorn.

One not so gloomy or down,
  And always quick to reverse a frown.

So, I walk outside with a thousand eyes on my back,
  Watching, and waiting for the universe's next attack.

And in the process of hating, it all,
  Do I dig a large ditch, for my inevitable fall.

So, I dance the fictitious dance,
  Of a happy, sane man at a glance.

I play the fiddler's chords,
As I, other's presence abhor.

But with all my fight and Vigor,
In the end am I a sore loser.

Because so smart am I in the world,
But if only I looked a little closer,

Would my inhibitions come unfurled.
For in a moment of understanding did I my ears perk.

As I heard a familiar musical work.
And all around me did I see.

People dancing and singing in melancholy.

In a moment of dread did they play,
A fiddle as they were caught in the fray.

Everyone hated everyone,

Everyone hated the universe.

Everyone adorned another deadly verse.

The land of hate was clearly seen,
In its entire glory and sheen.

And in a moment did I understand it all,
That everyone was going to share,

In the inevitable fall.

The hooded man calls

The hooded man calls,
  With a soothing voice, he whispers icy hope in my ears.

Hope and wishes and wonderful things,
  And most of all, an end to my biggest fears.

He places his arm over my shoulder as he laughs and jokes.
  And I grimace in the promised feelings of hope.

"Just a moment and you'll be free, don't you see?
  Of pain, of sadness and of melancholy."

"Would it hurt a lot?" I ask in apprehension.

"Is not the prospect of the contrary, worth it in the end?" He answers with conviction.

He finally moves in to place the traitor's kiss,
  But suddenly is my darkened heart filled with bliss.

As a light engulfs my universe,

A gentle hand guides mine, from the horrors of my internal verse.

With a gentle voice am I saved from the inquisitor,
From the hateful, dreadful, frequent visitor.

As I'm drawn from the darkness,

I fly.

I fly above the damned and the lost.
All of whom look like me,

Walking towards the land of hopes and joy and glee.

In a land of dread do we stop,
As the fair maiden, tightens her grip.

I search for words of gratitude,
Of hatred,
Something worth her short trip.

As I open my heart to speak,
Suddenly am I pulled into an embrace.

A terrible, horrible, engulfing....

Embrace.

I embrace my beautiful maiden back,

There in the land of dread did we make a pact.

One of pain, misery and tact.

One which surely,
My previously, non-existent future will impact.

For in the void of pain and misery,

That which is shared,
Can sometimes fill you with glee.

That which is understood,
Can set you free

And a fair maiden with a soft heart and beautiful soul,

Can keep you from giving the hooded man's words, any heed.

The immortal question

Do I live?

Have I lived?

With what can life be acquainted most,
  But misery.

Are we really alive?
  Is the next breath all that our little hearts for, strive?

Or is it joy?
  Does her existence, our heartbeat employ?

What was the other thing?

Ah yes, the feelings which bring the heart sting.

The feelings of love and peace,
  Do such feelings, our waking life appease?

Well, what more could I search for?

I've seen more than metaphor.

I've experienced all there is in the universe.
I've explored the depth and breadth of human verse.

I've seen galaxies being built by gods of time.
I've seen beauty in the supernovae which are far from sublime.

I'm eternal and I have seen every way,

I've heard every sound and I've said every say.

Yet still I sit and muse and think.

Yet still is my head pushed to the brink.
Isn't it ironic to see?

That it has taken me an eternity.

To understand the reason we live and die,
To find the goalpost at the end of the line.

But what more could I find after millennia of thought?

But the same old questions which I had all too easily forgot.

And with triumph in my voice, I shouted out loud.

'I've got the answer!!
To what can life be acquainted most, but with misery.'

Said I, as I stood proud.

Only to fall to my knees and cry.
  For in a search for the meaning of life.

This stupid poet had wasted an eternity.

This silly man had wasted a lifetime

They wait for the sun

I gazed at the dark sky,
  While waiting for the sun.

In a breath am I found, wanting.
  For what exactly?
  I do not know.

I want a need, that everyone has,
  I want to know; the inner sanctums of a heart.

A lover perhaps to find?
  Who may willingly lay in my tired arms,
  As we love one another for all time?

But I can't,

Or to be fair to my egoism.

I shan't.

I am too much of a stranger to my own heart,

To even motion towards my need for love.

To be fair had I a woman, my heart to hold,
Would I definitely be happy, greater or more bold?

Could I for a moment,
Her love cherish?
Or would I, pain and anguish on her life bestow?

In the search for love,
Could I truly trust,
That this poet's heart, shall not perish?

"I deserve this end, one all alone,
For what could I possibly find in love, if my heart is already so forlorn?"

Do I say, in that old,
Beaten, Saddened, bereaved tone.

Melancholy is my friend and she is the one I trust.

Because in the end is she real,
And not filled with apparitions of lust.

But even with all those thoughts swimming through an empty mind,
I still muse and think of what I, in a lover could find.

That would warrant my hand in hers,
Or justify my caress of her beautiful, dishevelled hair.

Or perhaps she thinks the same thing too,

And if she here was.

Would we be staring at so dark a night sky.

While waiting for the morning sun

They drink tea

I wake in the frosty morn,
  Here I hope for some peace to sojourn.

But turmoil and strife.
  Take over my mind.

Scratching, seething, biting.

Pandering, hoping, fighting

They all sit and have tea,
  The ones who give me company.

"Death, should you fear." Says one,

"No, to my counsel should you adhere." Interjects another.
  "Fear life, for the more you cling to it the more you lose, one day."

"Fear, everything, everyone?"
  I ask with a hopeless tone.

“Oh, this state, we very much condone” did they respond.

“But what of my opportunities for the day?” I ask in a softened tone.

“Isn’t this the reason you have our counsel summoned?” I heard them whisper

“You will, for melancholy, you will, for our hold on your thoughts” I heard another say

“Leave me be, just leave me be,” said I, as they laughed at me.
“We willed never to exist,
Let us a while here rest” said one slyly

“But you hurt me. You break me. You never stop....
Talking”

“We want to protect you; we want you to be safe from them,” said another

“We speak the truth, they speak lies.” Said one as if responding to my thoughts.

“Hope, joy and peace. They all will visit for a short while.
But they don’t hurt when they are here” said I to myself

“Yes, but they hurt when they leave,
We will always be here, what can you guarantee most but melancholy?”

Once more did I find myself,

Utterly at a loss for rebuttal.

What more could I do?

What more could I say?

How could I possibly hope to start the day?
So, I lay in bed, waiting for the council to adjourn.

Waiting for them to stop talking.

Hoping for some peace to sojourn....

The poet's plight

I cannot say,
   Who reads me today.

But I can say with certainty,
   There is a strange man who wrote me.

He watches and waits for a chance,
   As he once or twice steals an unholy glance.

He never hopes or prays,
   For a happy end to the day.

He's given up on a fairytale ending,
   But still finds the thought,

Nothing less than certain, or at least pending.

For the man who writes this poem has died,
   Not a transcendence passed the mortal realm.

But the seizure of the soul which is at his helm.

He doesn't know how else to say,
That maybe he just wants to be at peace one day.

But until then,
You will see.

That my words may sometimes be filled with glee,

Sometimes filled with pain.

Sometimes filled with scorn for the day.

But one thing always for certain will be.
That there will never be an end to me.

Words and verse and stories so sweet.

I always find a way,
For me, the dead ones to meet.

And in a few lines,
Of pitiful, wonderful, joyous rhyme.

I help this silly man for,
Some semblance of hope to find.

So, write away dead ones!

Write away oh sad ones!

I am verse and rhyme...

And today and forever shall my words transcend time.

The poet will day in vain.
But my words shall our future, forever sustain.

In my words are all poets immortal,

So write,

Write,

Write Away.

And hope that I will share your words with the living,

Someday.

They stare at their feet

'Pessimism, the modern ethos, married to our souls and made up of nothing'

I cannot recall where I had this saying heard.
  But I'm sure that, at the time did I find it quite absurd.

The thought of nothing and soul.
  Had not yet filled me with woe.

But one day did I look up to see.
  Everyone staring at their own feet, as they walked past me.

While the shadows plagued the streets and walkways.

The walkers just walked their own way.

Of the modern age.
  I called for some hope,

I begged for some redemptive tome.

But in the end did I find myself, utterly alone.

'Something is wrong, something is not right.'

'How could I,
Not have seen the beginning of our plight?'

For in a moment did they turn,
The masters of the universe who live in the valley of thorns.

And with evil breath did they screech,
As they made their way towards me.

"Alone, alone I perish.
For I have ceased.
To stare listlessly at my feet."

"Woefully, woefully I trod,
For I had not that evil memory forgot.

Of the old man by the sea, who looked from his feet,
To talk to me.

And in a woeful tone said,"

'Mourn the modern age,
For hope is dead.
And the end will hold none of it in the morning'

As he walked away did I remember him saying with a grunt.

'Pessimism,

The modern ethos,

Married to our souls and made up

Of nothing.'

The land of the living

I sleep for several hours,
  Before getting into bed.

In a moment I wake and find myself,
  Far from the dead.

With fairies and knights,
  All brewing delight.

And the stories of valour and victory,
  Which for a moment, held my sight.

Until suddenly was my vision pilfered,
  By a being which had my heart lifted.

She stood before me and said.
  'How was it, in the land of the dead?'

I searched for an answer but couldn't speak.
  For enamoured was I by the princess before me.

'Who are you? What's your name?'
I finally stammered after trying again.

'My name is a name you know well'
Said she in the tone of a friend.

'Forget about that, let's hope and pray.'
'That a brave knight shall this way come to save me this day.'
Said the princess

'From whom shall this knight Save you?' Said I in shock
'Are you not already free?'

'Free to reign in the land full of joy,
But never one who has seen the sea'
Said she with a forlorn heart.

The look of which tore my soul apart.

With outstretched hand did I behest,
To this beautiful princess's quest.

And together did we march,

Onward! To the West.

In a moment, however, was it all covered,

By tendrils of death which had finally my location, discovered.

And in the air were we flung,

Hand in hand as the whirlwind's trial had begun.

'They beckon for me, the dying ones.' Said I in a hopeless tone

'Well, such an end could I not condone,' said she.
Slowly as her hands clutched to my shoulders and arms.

With the force from beyond was I ripped from the land of the gods.

'Once more I ask, what is your name?'
'Tell me now before I leave, for I may never be back again.'
Said I, as further I fell, into the black abyss.

'Stay strong and remember hence, the name of this beautiful princess'

I am 'love' and one day will you see.

That by My hands, shall I set you free.

But first I hope and pray, that you, this debt will repay

And search for me, brave knight
Beg for my hold on your life.
And find me... One day in the land of strife.

In the land of decay.

In the land from which you may not escape.

In the land where you have lost your way.

In the sordid, terrible, haunting,

Seething, abhorrible....

Land of the Dead’

The fated night

My strength had left my soul,
  My Armor had many a hole.

I leaned on a tree hoping for the embrace,
  Of the fair one's cold tendrils, who around me shall lace.

'A life of toil' I whisper to my heart.
  'A life of strife' I say as I, with my balance, do part.

'Who is this knight, which this way lay?' Heard I a woman say.

'Who is this knight who hath lost his way?' Did her words, my strength betray.

'A Dead knight, for here I lay.' said I to the woman.
  'A knight whose country, his life hath betray!'

'That's no good chivalrous knight.'

'You have many a person to save this night.' Said the woman with a voice so sweet yet filling me with fright.

'You speak to a dead knight, woman of virtue.'
'I beg of you let another; your safety ensure.' Said I with a withered soul, Void of fight.

'No woman so fair, so kind and so sweet should their sight on me set.
For mine, is the sight of the dead.' Said I,
as I sit against a tree.

'Well, then I pray thee brave knight, not a sight on me to set.
For mine is the sight of scorn and hate.' Said she as closer she came.

In the silent moonlight did we each other betray,
As with eyes set on one another could we finally our hearts obey.

And finally, did I see,
The wonderous creature standing before me.

Before this knight stood a fae, void of a wing.

Before the fae, slumped a knight who in battered armour sat,
For he, war, had seen.

I tried to stand up, but as I got to my feet.
Did my legs giveaway from under me.

As I fell, I was caught midway.
By the beautiful, one-winged fae.

And after a moment of silence,
Did she with a soothing voice,
To my heart say.

"Your life I gladly take in my arms,

For this did you readily give away.

No more shall you, in this sordid armour lay.

No more will you die, for you are in the arms of a fae."

"And void of wing may you be,
But your wing shall I be."

Said I as my armour fell,
And with it,
So did my melancholy.

"To you my fae, shall I my life for an eternity betray"...

"And for you, kind knight, shall I my heart, parlay"....

The cloud.

A cloud takes flight every evening,
And returns every morn.

Beckoning to the call of the illusion,
And adhering to hopeless exclusion.

Hoping to spread the threat of sight.
For what do I see when I close my eyes, but the absence of light?

And what do I in mourning excite,
When I such thoughts in my heart ignite?

So, my mind runs a marathon ahead of my plight.

Measuring the goals of my future,
Begging for the end of my fight.

I have no hope to be,
One so free of melancholy.

I have no arm to hold,

Or love which turmoil can behold.

So, I close my eyes,

Waiting to be light,

Waiting for the waves,
To put an end to my plight.

The end I hold with great jeer,
Especially as my end draws near.

And in a moment without cause,

Am I a free man, void of pain.

Void of any cosmic sores.

As brittle as glass.

The cloud which I adorn....

As beautiful and deadly, as the void of scorn.

The cloud which takes flight every eve.

And returns every morn.

The eve's song

The evening song calls...

The evening song calls...

As I Wade through the bog of misery,

Wishing as I will,
  Dreaming as I might,

For an illusion of chivalry.

For the hope of grace so white.

I toil and beg for rest,
  I hope and pray for night.

I cease to put my strength to the test,
  Lest my hope be pulled to a villainous jest.

Or my joy return to a hopeless, uncanny sight.

So, I crawl to my doorstep aloft,

And slowly cower into my safe little raft.

Open the bedding once and for all,

And once more hope and pray to attend to....

The evening Songs call....

The man

I met a man the other day who gave me a fright,
For a while, the very thought of him kept me up at night.

The smell of death on his clothes,
Sent me cowering in a homely abode.

The look of misery in his eyes,
Did the memory I hope never to reprise.

'Curse the day as you curse others with your life' he scorned,
With the voice of the wise and adorned.

'And never to trust another with your miserable life' he whispered,
In the sickly tone of a friend who held a scythe.

I turned to run away. I hoped to leave this man.
But before I could leave,

He asked with a slithering grin.

"What's my name, my friend?"

"No, I will not say it!" I exclaimed.
I willed not, to answer the man of sin.

"Answer, lest I more pain on your soul append." He said again

"The man" I uttered as I hoped, death some relief for me would send.

"The man who in the mirror dwells and begs" he responded.

"The man in the mirror who is my friend"

The ceiling

An empty ceiling,
An icy morn.

I wait in my bed,
For my heart,
Some excitement to adorn.

A start of the new day,
Beckoning my soul for hope.

That perhaps, just maybe.

I might find a chance to elope.
From the humdrum so arduous and plain.

Searching for the rushing of blood,
Which flows through my veins.

At the sight of the slightest inconvenience,
Can I a terrible fate foresee.

At the brink of exhaustion,
Do I not beg for peace and glee?

So, I wish for change and forgo melancholy,
By searching for dreams and hoping to be free.

But alas what do I know?
A man feeling so empty and worn.

All I see before me for now,

Is an empty ceiling...

And an icy morn....

Eternity

Do I know you?
Have I seen your face?

In your eyes do I feel the tugging of a lover's embrace.

Whisper sweet nothings in my ear.

Hold me closer my dear.

Let this dream never end,
Oh! For us, forever to spend.

Sitting and speaking and laughing and crying,

Forever beautiful...

Forever undying...

But for now, I wait alone,
To hear you calling on the phone.

To tell you about my day,
  Or agonising on what to say.

One day will I, a loving heart find,
  With whom I shall myself bind.

And together, forever shall we be.

Today, tomorrow and for all eternity.

"Aren't I so happy?"

Oh, for a moment of illusion,
　What would I give?

To sit without confusion,
　Or the beckoning of a hollow grave.

I wait for the morning sun,
　Hoping to take in some joy,

But all I feel is despair, in immense employ.

I guess pain is the price for truth,

Which I in abundance have.
　Because once I was full of hope,
　Back then, however, was I glad.

To partake in the fruitless fight,
　To keep my soul in the light.

But easily did I see,

That the shadows never leave.

So, give me an illusion bright,
 So warm and so free,
 And discard my feelings of strife, pain and melancholy.

Give me a beautiful morning without an empty heart.

And a lover for my soul so that we may never part.
 And until my greedy heart wants for more, will I say in glee.

"Aren't I so happy.

Aren't I so happy?"

The cafeteria of delight.

What would you like?

In the cafeteria of delight?

A hopeless thought of melancholy?

Or a cup of pessimistic fright?

Because after every delight am I found wanting.

And after every purchase,
  Do I find the morn, ever more,

Daunting.

I work to feed myself in the cafeteria of delight...

But in the end, I eat alone...

And am quickly sent home...

Where the damp walls call for sickness,
  And the shadows beg for access.

Take me back to that cafeteria of delight.

So that I may eat for a short while and return to the

World of spite.

The Fright

I find myself walking on a narrow road,
  As I walk, I beg for a warm abode.

I see homes baked in holy light

As I walk,

I stand upon the street in terror,
  On this cold wintery night.

For suddenly was I affright....

When I realised,
  Surely,
  Something was not right....

For truly,
  Before me,

Happy smiles and faces did I see.

But what was that?

Truly,
Staring back at me?

Dark strings filled with fear,
Had in jest,
Themselves, their presence leer.

For once my eyes were opened thus,
Did I see who was controlling us.

Dark figures cloaked in pain.

Who hope for the world to obtain.

Yet how silly of me not to see.

The figure,

Whose dark puppety

Strings......

Were controlling me.

Take the chance!

Why do I know your warmth, though I've never laid in your arms?

Why have I memorised your laughter though I've never heard you speak?
  I am still yet, enraptured by your charms.

But I have heard you laugh, and I have felt your touch.

'There you are!' She exclaimed,
  As she pulled me into an encompassing embrace.

A warmth I know very well,
  A voice I can swear to the Lord,
  I have surely felt.

'Let's go! Follow me!' She says as she tugs at my heart.
  As her hand in mine,
  Never does part.

I follow her into a deep forest,

Wading through thorns and thistles.
And wooden shard.

They cut and poke and prod my soul,
But I follow her nonetheless.
For she has taken my heart.

We enter a clearing and speechless do I see.

A mountain range sitting before me.

And with a gesture, I could never forget,
Do I feel the touch of a gentle peck.

'I have to go now, I love you!' She says,

As I lurch to grab her hand.

But suddenly I find the morning rays.

As she disappears from my sight like falling sand.

Her embrace replaced with a morning frost,

And her laughter with ghostly silence,
Has ultimately been lost.

'How could I go on without you!' I exclaim.

'In a dream did I make myself known' I heard a beautiful voice say

'It's up to you to find me on your own.'

'I'm waiting for you my love, one day soon,

You will see,

That I will never depart from thee.'

The lovers plight

A haunted hand,
Caresses a lonely heart.

With its elegant movements,
It hopes for the heart,
From some sadness to part.

The heart cries out in shame,
As in hopeless reprieve,
Does it feel naught but pain.

As the shrill screams fill the air,
When their eyes are singed,
By the sight of another nightmare.

One with no infernal end,
One which shivers down one's spine,
Does surely send.

As the feelings of death,
With bony fingers,

Encroach upon his heart.

As their hands,
Though cursed, Hope,
From melancholy to part.

For horror to cease,
As love plays its final part.
In this unholy piece of art.

So once more is he left to beg,
Not for want of love,
But that of dread.

As a cold heart hopes to be warmed,
As the whispering willows,
Have their final warnings,
Warned.

Beg for love, oh woman of scorn!
For as you are tied to a rack and are torn,
Shall you, its immortal presence, mourn.

Hope for love young man!
As you are beaten by an inquisitor,
though your heart yearns for love to understand.

Love is amazing and wonderful and free,
But the rotting muses never said,
That it was free of melancholy.

So, embrace eternal death once more,
As your musty love,
Is all you shall dance for.

In the eyes of a lover,
Filled with empty sockets,
And bony embrace,

As only in your nightmares,
Could you, a warm lover,
Ever hope to face.

And sing a song of sordid love,
To the Holy Lord,
Who resides in the heavens above.

And receive nothing but silence,
Because true beautiful love,
Is nought but unholy penance thus.

Of the shivering weakness,
Found within all of us,

And for some people, it is plain to see,
That this deathly weakness is nought else,
But sordid, hopeful, melancholy.

So once more I warn,

Love, your lover dearly,
And love them forevermore,

But never forget this,
Your first love's Icy, deathly kiss,
For her name was melancholy,

And one day will she carry her eternal love,
On the wings of a raven,
As your puppet's strings shall finally be cut.

And your life will she end with this.

Sending you to the middle,
Of that dark abyss.

While embracing your bony heart,
As she promises never,
From you to part,

And with one final, selfish wish,

Shall she end your life with this,

As together you shall embrace,

Enraptured eternally,

By true love's final,

Horrific,

Bony Kiss.

Death's dance

The screeching of a siren,
  As the worried ones,
  Run and hide.

I find myself hoping for a moment of peace,
  On which my old weary heart,
  Could abide.

They cower in fear in their homes,
  As the sun hopes to confide.

With the will of devils,
  Who by destruction,
  Will abide.

Hiding,
  Cowering,
  Shivering,
  Covered in sweat,

Men losing their minds,

As their hoarse voices,
Scream to their last breath.

Women cowering in fear,
As their last tear,
Is finally, wept.

They beg to be saved,
To an iron god,
Their end, hoping not to accept.

And of the children?
The children smile,
For the silly men screamed and the funny women wept.

They laugh in misunderstanding,
As the truth from them is kept.

In the heart of death,
On a small street,
Hoping for some rest.

I find a peculiar sight,
Of which my heart,
Can attest.

A man and woman,
Embroidered with hopeless smile,
As they, their final tears had wept.

But in a horrid display of hope,

Did they hand in hand,
Their final end accept.

The end to this mortal realm.
As they danced and wept.

Two lovers in the thrall of noiseless dance,

As finally,
The gods,
Delivered their golden Lance.

And as the land was cleansed,
By holy fire.

The two lovers danced.
Hand in hand,

They danced.

Once more to love in life,

Once more to steal a lover's glance,

At the love of the melancholic,

Who in death shall dance.

The dead man's reprise

The dark clouds hug the horizon,
  Like a mother's embrace on a quiet night.

The shadows dance in the icy moonlight,
  As the nightmares beg for reprise.

What is there to see in the dark?
  Except for shadows who call for our demise.

Except for the cold, icy embrace of melancholy.

Except for the misery,
  Of the wise.

Give in to the encompassed embrace,
  Lest you in hope shall lie.

For truth lies in hopelessness,
  For at least she, shall not lie.

So, I wake once more to the horrid embrace of life,

To walk once more in misery and strife.

To beg for an end to hope which lies,
In the song of the dead man's reprise.

The haunting night

The call of the dead,
Beckons the heart to feel,

More than eternal dread.
As incantations are uttered,
Better, never to have been unsealed.

As the shadows murder and steal,
You stir In your bed.
For your mind, shall be their next meal.

Close the door,
Lock it tightly,
Apply a holy wax seal,

Stay from the windows,
And beg for the day,
Nightly.

The shadows shall give you no rest,

And my sleepless heart,
Can hitherto attest.

For the damned ones hope to seek,
To break the hearts of the meek.
As your gaze deeper into the abyss, do peak.

The beautiful and the clean.
Are rend from life,
By the actions of the unseen.

Devils and angels plague the night.
And hitherto you will find a cosmic fight.

As souls are cleaved from the light,
By the actions of those,
Who believe they are eternally right.

As the night is filled with the shrilled screams,
Of empty husks of Men and women,
Who in shuffled walk plague the night.

So, beg for the day,
And beg for the light.

Because nought but bony evil,
Hooded and clandestine,
In the company of devils,

And immortal shadow,
Drunk on heresy and wine,

Haunt,

Your eternal,

Night.

An ode to lovesickness

Oh, woman of virtue,
  Which o'er went.

Why must I long for you so?

Why must my heart be rend?

I beg for a chance,
  For you to grace my heart,
  With one more doe-eyed glance,

But I'm left utterly alone,
  From my balance have I part.
  relegated to a broken stance.

My armour, tattered and torn,
  As my heart is pierced with a holy lance.
  As my soul is now with sadness, adorn.

Some fools call it love,

Others madness,
Others eternal scorn.

All that my simple heart knows,
Is that it feels more than forlorn,
reeling in more than sadness.

I want to feel your caress,
I want for your heart to adorn.
Over my black heart of stone,

As my heart forevermore,
In disheartened sonnet,
To love will atone.

But wanting am I found,
As I look at my heart on the ground.
As I am buffeted by the tumultuous sea.

Because foolish was I not to see,

The melancholy found,

In my eternal love for thee.

The arms of a woman

Do I confer my love to thee?
Or will my heart in sadness,
Choose to flee?

Do I share my sadness with you,
Or will the rain clouds,
Spoil the value of a romantic view?

A serene field,
Filled with holy light,
As the worries of the world are sealed.

Sealed, are they?
Or in a hopeless laugh filled with plight,
Do they to the god of madness pray?

2 hopeless romantics in love,
Will always,
In earnest, search for the tears of a dove.

But perhaps this time,
We will be saved,
By a mutual love for the Lord above.

Well mutual, I may say,
But my love for a lord,
Is never easy when I've lost my way.

But still, I hope and pray,
To the Iron God,
Who from love, will not stray.

Perhaps this once I can dream,
As I tentatively,
Hope for some peace to glean.

From slender fingers,
Rose-kissed lips And a woman's gaze,
That scorches my heart to cinders

So another day do I wait,
As my heart longs,
To finally clear its rotting slate.

For my dreams to begin,
As my cold, musty heart,
Has been lost to the ultimate fate.

Of disorganised love and attachment,
Which only adds more moss,
To my ethereal slate.

But alas mere words do I write,
I have given in to love,

I have lost my fight.

As I hope and pray,
To find a better end,
To this infernal day.

Crying as I do,
For in the embrace of nothing,
I spend my mortal nights.

As a soft tear-soaked pillow do I find,
And a gentle caress of pain,
As sadness to my rotting heart does bind.

As her sweet voice pulls me into the abyss,
"You are mine, my love," she says,
As her words are laced with that of an enchantress.

Once more to fly,
In the land of death,
Once more to finally die,

In the arms of a mare,
In the eyes of a doe,
In the heart of one who is truly mine.

The confession

What more than love, can destroy the walls of a heart?
 In earnest hope and care,
 You render me weak, hoping from love, never to part.

A romantic of a man writes this poem,
 In earnest, he writes,
 Hoping for some love to condone.

He writes this poem to say,
 'I am enamoured,
 Into your arms, do I wish to lay.'

To dance the dance of eternal love,
 As we watch the horizon, hand in hand,
 As we fly on the wings of a dove.

I wish to caress your hand,
 I wish to hold you close,
 Such wishful imagery, can my heart not withstand.

But none more, than to hear your voice,
To see your eyes, looking back in mine,

As we sing, dance and dine,
As we find ourselves in love for all of time.

As he dreams a pleasant dream,
One he wishes to share with you,
One that fills the heart with serene,

Of the beautiful doe-eyed lady fair,
Who in earnest beauty,
Can to none other, compare.

As he falls in love with that which is unseen,
For all love hitherto,
Could never compare, to the love I feel for you.

A strange dichotomy of thought,
As all my logic in a swift swoop,
Is brought to naught.

But a weak attempt at understanding you,
Is my search herein fraught,
In this mortal verse,

As I hope to see the universe,
Sitting on a throne of love,
And ask her, what is truly true?

And in a swift moment does she reply,

You,
The beautiful woman of virtue.

The woman with whom I have stumbled to a fall,
With whom my love,
Is overflowing with enthral.

So now I shall write that which burns my heart,
As I hope for, from your loving arms,
Never to have to part.

With this shall I my heart parlay,
In a confession letter,
I love you, and this do I wish to convey.

And if you, a knight will save,
Then this too shall he promise,
That his love for you will never change.

So, if you will,
Lady Fair,
Shall we love away?

And hope that one day,
We listen to an eternal song of love,
As we dance the night away?

An eternal waltz of beauty and heart,
Of which, from each other's arms,
Do I wish never to part,

And that is all that this lovestruck poet,
  wishes to say,

That I truly love you,

And I really wouldn't have it any other way.

The shadows dance

A glimmer of hope,
Pierces the misty dark,
As the shadows dance,

And sing their songs of joy,
With magical, broken harp.

The skeletons waltz,
The waltz of mossy doom,
As the dead ones sing,

And the music never halts,
Nor ceases to begin,

As the enchanting, ethereal melody,
All but consumes.

There is no mortal end,
But that of sordid sin.

To the ones who live in strife,
  And odes to evil do sing,

As they, blood do pour,
  In cups lined with blasphemy,
  While drinking with delight.

But enamoured by lust is man,
  And so too is he with fright,

As he seeks devils in the shadows,
  Shivering in terror,
  In the middle of the night.

As he sings songs to their praise,

And prayer for their plight.

But such drivel has never a shadow enthralled,
  As the soul of a lost one crying in pain,
  The echoes which their presence does call.

And in a hungry song of plight do they sing,
  Not to feast on the dead,
  But to call their kin.

As the children cry in fear,
  And the men and women shed a tear.

So stay not out at night young one,
  And beware of sounds far and near.

They come in peaceful scurry promising fun.

As the shadows and skeletons feast.
On the bones of the living,
Devouring the innocent like a beast.

And still, they will dance,
An ode to death,
They shall dance.

And once more they will sing.
A song with no begin,
They shall sing.

As the night begins to fade,

And the birds sing their holy serenade.

For now,
Once more can you sigh,
For you have survived the night.

But prepare for the cosmic score,
And make sure to lay scripture,
Upon your wooden floor.

As again the songs of death will ring out.

Calling the creatures of scorn,
To worship and praise the end,
As they sing and cry,

For they have no choice to be,
And to this end are they never free,
For they frolic in the land of death.

But after every dusk do they emerge,
To sing and cry in delight,
screeching in the middle of the night.

Their song upon your heart to score,
As they beg to be free of death,
But bereaved are they found.

As they are forced to dance forevermore.

Death's ode to life

The quiet eve,
Wrought with death,
As you a heavy breath do heave,

wincing at every shadow,
As your mind races,
To find an end to sorrow,

Beg not for peace,
For the dead ones beg,
hoping that their torment would someday cease.

But lest you heed their call,
You must keep strong,
For your misery is their enthral.

The swiftness of breath leaving a corpse,
Delights the lips of those,
Who cannot hope to feel remorse.

But hate them not,
 Instead,
 Despise their lot.

For dead are they,
 And lest you see,
 They are also filled with melancholy.

Strife and misery,
 Love and insanity.

Yes, though they are dead,
 They live forevermore,
 To make you shiver in your bed.

And though they cannot drink,
 They feast and wail in delight,
 As another man hopelessly takes his life.

So cover yourself in your sleep,
 And hope and pray that you are blessed to be,
 The ones whom this shadow cannot see.

The ones who are prone to peace,
 The ones adorned,
 With a multi-coloured fleece.

Pray that the shadows will leave you be,
 As you wince in your sleep,
 From a nightmare so deep,

A nightmare,
  That is truly free.

When compared to the misery,
  You hopelessly feel,
  In the shadows of your melancholy.

An ode to misery

I held onto her in joy,
  As I hoped for words unknown,
  To wordlessly employ,

She winced at my touch,
  And held me tight,
  In hopeless reprieve did she not say much.

For she knew of my impending blight,
  As she contemplated the agony I shall feel,
  On my terribly lonely nights.

"My love, I fear I must leave now",
  She said, as her tender voice filled me with dread.

'Why should you leave me now?'
  I asked as my face was strewn with furrowed brow.

'I must leave now, my love' she said,
  as she floated with the wings of a dove.
  Floating high above my head.

'Now you must love another'
she said as I stood up in a worried huff.

'A new mistress I give thee',
Said she,
'And her name is melancholy'

'My sister fair'
She said,
'My sister who is eternally bare'

'but 'happiness' my love, why must you leave?'
I cried as my heart started to sting with melancholy.

'A short while will I be gone but sadness my sister, has really done no wrong'
said she in a tone forlorn.

'Love her please' She begged, as my heart with sadness,
Was stained red.
'And you shall see'

'That my sister is also in need of love,
Even if her name is Misery'

'Love her I shall, my dear' said I in melancholy.

For none can love her as much as me.
And even if her name is misery

I shall show her the love of one,

Who in sadness and bereave,
loves with a broken heart for surely is he free.

In earnest, she vanished,
Leaving my heart cold,
Dead and famished.

As a new mistress made herself known,
With the crack of a whip,
Did she sadness condone.

She tears at my soul as she says,
'Worthless are you,
you didn't deserve my sister fair'

'To the ends of despair with you weakling!
Not even your tears deserve my care!'
Said she in a saddened tone,

As an image of her own pain,
Did she try to withhold.

But love her I shall,
And this I declared to happiness my love,
For though she had to leave as a child.

I will love her forevermore.
Misery, happiness and melancholy.

If I can love such a mistress,
Then I shall truly be free.

Lament not my life oh happy ones,
   For Happiness is your mistress for a time.

One day will we reunite,

And such a day will be nothing short of divine.

Until then,
   I bide my time,
   In the arms of the sullen lover,

On whom misery does dine.

And I wait forevermore,

For happiness, my true love to find.

Sadness her name

Sadness is her name,
For she lays the floor bare,
With her sorrowful pain.

She winces and wails,
She stammers in short breath,

As her sister Happiness, is longed for,
As the wordless need for love,
Is never met.

Sadness is her name,
She seeks not peace,
Not even a semblance of fame.

She wants to be loved,
And elevated on the shoulders of her beloved,
To be closer to the stars above.

But alone is she found,
Not singing a lovers song,

But crying hopelessly on the ground.

As her clothes are soaked wet,
With the tears of her lovers,
Who wait to leave her with bated breath.

I look into her eyes as she wails,
She sees my heart,
And her resolve quickly fails.

For I shall devote myself to her,
Though she may cry,
To her will I, my love confer.

Though scarred and saddened is she,
I will be the one,
To ease her melancholy.

For have you not heard the tale of old?
Misery loves company,
And my company is with a lover's kiss behold.

So I hold her in my arms,
Sadness being her name,
As I listen to her qualms.

And she gives me a softened smile,
Not one of happiness, her sister,
But a want of alms.

As I give her my life,

And stain her heart with my charms,
As I make this woman my eternal wife.

The first and last lover of sadness was I,
And for this title,
Am I prepared to someday die.

To see her cry a little less,
As she lays my head upon a sullen altar,
Singing a song as I drift into eternal rest.

To wander the earth once more,
To be beaten and bruised,
And cursed forevermore.

But as her lover, I will say,
That her saddened soul,
Is truly worth dying for at the end of the day.

The lover's lament

I walk the cobblestone bare,
As the gaslit lamps,
Reveal a lady fair.

Closer I had dared to trod,
Her eyes filled with terribly saddened tear,
Waiting for the intervention of an iron god.

As her hands gripped to life,
While gazing at the stars,
As her hands gripped a small knife.

Her eyes filled with hope,
And her fingers trembling,
As she aimed the blade at her delicate throat,

Bewildered was she,
As her eyes scanned the fog,
Looking for a handsome lover in this unholy bog.

Closer I trod,
As with a swift movement,
Did I, her weapon stop.

'Why wish you to die, lady fair?'
Asked I with a sadness that could not compare.

'I wish to die in want of love',
Said she with the tone of an angel above.

'Love say you? But what love is there for a dead maiden?'
Said I before continuing.
'I can see your heart is heavily laden'

'I wish for blood on this stone to be strewn'
Said she,
'For no man wants a broken maiden, and this is my ultimate doom'

I threw her knife to the side,
As I embraced her close,
'I can see your pain and this can I not condone'

Said I in a soft, subtle tone.
'I shall love you dearly'
Said I as my eyes were teary.

'A life you have given away'
Said I.
'And today you have surely died'

'For in my arms shall you forever, your sullen tears hide'
Said I,
As in her shoulder did I my tears confide.

'Today I have surely died good sir'
Said she as her tears, she surely did hide.
'And my love shall I hold for you, it shall never stir'

That day surely a woman had died,
And in my arms,
Shall she forever, her sullen tears confide.

As I caress her soul with my hands,
As her pain,
Will I always understand.

But forever will we be,
Together as lovers,
clinging to one another in our melancholy.

And one day shall we wed,
As her heart shall she lay,
Before the man who sings of the dead.

I love her, that lady in red,
For though her hands tremble,
And she lay in dread.

She is mine lover,

And she, shall I surely wed.

It's all in good fun

The sorrowful lament of a girl,
Breaks the bounds of time,
As her shrill shriek does the heart unfurl.

She begs for a way home,
For an end to terror,
For a final forgotten tome.

But silence is her friend,
Well, not silence,
But tears which to the ground are sent.

In a sorrowful tone,
She cries tears of heartbreak,
Tears of immortal woe,

'Oh, misery my eternal foe'

And yet, the tears keep falling,
The day never ceasing,

As the dead ones in jest are calling.

'Happiness is fleeting,
So too is pain,
Even though tears leave upon my sullen heart, eternal stain.'

On the rosy lips of a dame,
As she cries and laments,
As she hopes to survive the haunting quiet of this refrain.

So once more she lay,
On the edge of a never-ending abyss,
On a fateful day.

Hoping to save another in her womanly arms,
Hoping for a lover who,
Her eternal suffering shall take away.

But none ever cometh,
The dead ones in jest sing with joy,
As her sullen pain, they do covet,

They laugh and wail,
In their haunting laughter,
They hope for some delight to attest.

In the heart of the loveless one,
In the tears of the saddened one,
As she laughs a hopeless laugh,

As her head is finally laid to rest,

And her eternal suffering,
In hopeless laughter is wrung.

From her cold body,
Which shivers violently,
upon the gentle caress of a loving touch.

Yet still, she waits and wails,
Now too,
She waits and wails,

For her lover to come,
For her eternal friend,
With her soul to become one,

With the woman on the run,
From that which can come undone,

As the shadows jest at her pain,
As they revel in her tears and say,

It's all in good fun....

It's all in good fun....

In the arms of a lover

Beg forevermore,
As your hope and love,
Are strewn upon the rotting floor.

As your heart laments the chance for life,
As your rotting heart,
Begs for a hint of strife.

Thus, the shadows sing,
Not in want of peace,
But that of sin.

As they hope for your heart to bereave,
As they destroy everything,
And only sadness in your life does leave.

Beg for some peace,
Beg for some reprieve,
As the doomed ones, their jesting never cease.

To see to it that your heart is troubled,
To make you fall to your knees,
Hoping that you, at their feet would grovel.

And when they jeer,
With shiny white teeth filling your heart with disdain,
They will cackle in eternal cheer.

But the shadows will die,
As you in a lover's arms do lie,
For their warmth shall your mortal light maintain.

As the life returns to a dead man's corpse.
As you hope to find an end to that immortal curse.

But beware young one,
For as you leave,
The embrace of a lover in hopeful reprieve.

In a moment of weakness will you find,
The shadows reinvigorated,
As they hope upon your heart to dine.

So leave not her arms,
Young lad,
Lest you lose your peaceful calm.

Break not his embrace,
Young lass,
Lest your heart come to terrible harm.

Cling to your lover,
With white-knuckled hope,
Cling.

For the end of the shadows and their kin,
Will in your lovers' arms,
Ultimately begin.

So cling.
And cling forever more.

And never hurt your heart,
As in the absence of a lover,
Will the shadows hunt you to the moor.

And in a moment, a shrill screech will ring out,
Piercing the quiet night,
As the bony ones reveal their claws.

And in a hopeless shriek, you will find,
The warm embrace of your husband,
Or the slender arms of your bride.

And suddenly you will see,
The end of your sorrow,
In this tumultuous cosmic sea.

As your lover will break your hidden seal,
So once more dear child,
In the arms of another will you finally feel.

That a true fairytale ending,
  Is ultimately real.
  In the land void of joy trapped by holy seal.

And your silly fears of shadows and demons,
  Were all but forced to kneel,
  Before the strength of your lover's touch.

And the feelings of love and peace,
  You shall finally feel.

As your lover's shoulders will catch your tear,
  And hope will take the place of fear

The nightmare will finally cease,
  With the kind eyes of your lover gazing back into yours,
  As finally now and forevermore,

Will you know peace.

The shared nightmare

Why must I, love so fear?

As I in my heart,
  Hold the memory of womanly warmth,
  Of rosy lips which I hold dear?

Why must my sullen heart tear?

And by unholy light,
  Be burnt and seared?

Why must it be gripped by fear?

Oh to love freely,
  This do I wish,

But to hate only,
  This is all this sullen poet,
  May hope to accomplish.

Not hate of the mortal,
  Nor a lady fair.

But the dank musty room,
  That contorts in strange ways,
  As it comes to you in quiet nightmares.

Filled with echoed droplets that,

Drip,

Drip,

Drip.

And in the centre will you find,
  An ungodly,
  Unholy abyss.

Without a window in sight,
  As you are plunged into eternal night.

But still, could you perceive,
  The chance to end it all,

As the sound of a bony tap on the floorboards,
  Fills the night,
  With a noise that fills the shadows with delight.,

The darkness enthrals,
  At that eternal choice.

The chance to make it right.
  As the abyss calls for one more man,
  To step out of the light.

As gravity, its way does make,
  For what was rotting land.

Indeed I plunge,
  Headlong,
  Into the darkness, I lunge.

For though her sight fills me with glee,
  Afterwards, I feel naught,

But terrible, lonely melancholy.

To this end,
  Is my love truly not free.

As I wait on the edge of a misty pier,
  Gazing into a frothing, tumultuous sea.

Waiting for a lover to behold,
  And if I may be so bold.

Perhaps a pretty princess,
  Or a beautiful lady fair,
  With which I can share.

In this eternal nightmare.

As our hearts are intertwined,
Recklessly with unholy care.

With her bony fingers caressing mine head,
As her fleshless lap,
Do I make my eternal bed.

As her bony fingertips gently caress my head,
Her loving skeletal teeth,
Smile in earnest with nary a look of dread.

For a moment,
I begged of her.

That in matte fleshless arms,
Bound by white sinew,
I may solemnly rest my head.

And so too will my vision be,

So filled with mossy wood,

And uncertainty,

As in a beautiful tone of dread does she say,

'Be still my love, for in my caress,
Do you spend your last day.'

And in a moment of shivering solace.
With a tender caress void of malice.

Do I find,
  A hopeful rest in the arms of a lady,
  Who gazes at my heart as her ultimate dine.

Though bony,
  Broken,
  And void of strife,

In this woman's arms,

Am I willing to pledge my life.

So with absolute trust,

I rest my head,

As I slowly,

Drift away.

A lady fair, in torment

Who are you Lady Fair?
Who wakes in the night,
To another shattering nightmare?

The woman of fear,
Who never sees the light,
Though she searcheth both far and near.

As with melancholy, she sheds a tear,
The shadows which o'er dwell,
In the valley of immortal fear.

Beckon her tender heart,
As their bony tendrils,
With sickly laughter leer.

As their horrid slithery tone,
Play their seething, scraping part.

Tattered, scarred and void of a heart,
She wanders the midnight road,

Hoping for death to play his final part.

As their breath fills with dread,
As their love is filled,
With the metallic taste of the dead.

She winces at their call,
For they never cease to beckon,
Conveying A promise of an easy, whimsical fall.

She clutches her head in misery,
As the shadows multiply in a whisper,
As in her tears do they find their enthral.

She sees an apparition of an unknown mister,
Sneering, pearly white teeth filled with rot,
With a musty handshake that adds to her lot.

With a ghostly smile does he promise her,
The secrets of the universe,
And the end to sordid human verse,

He indeed promises all this.

To entice,
To flaunt,
To give her debaucherous thirst.

And in return a small price to pay,
Just with her whole heart,
Must she eternally part.

In a box with a neat bow,
  Must she her soul ultimately,
  Parlay.

The shadows seem so fair,
  When dank, dark, musty darkness,
  Is held in compare.

But strong she holds her mind,
  As one day a lover,
  Does she hope to find

One who wills for her heart to ensnare,
  A lover who one day,
  For her heart shall surely care.

And unlike this evil nightmare,
  Will her true lover,
  Treat her kindly.

Loving her dearly,
  With tenderness and care,

Cherishing her beauty and elegance,
  Hugging her and holding her close,
  While gently caressing her dishevelled hair.

Expressing his love for her,
  His arms to call her own,
  In a moment his love with an embrace to confer.

A final end to her unholy nightmare.
  A chance for love finally,
  With a tentative touch, to play fair.

And forevermore will they love,
  As he with his own heart, does part,
  To the beautiful lady fair.

And once more is the heart,
  In a neat little bow,
  Parlayed.

But half the heart of a man,
  And half the heart of a woman,
  This time was paid.

As they place their hearts on the line,
  In final,
  Holy matrimony,

Filled with laughter,
  And Beautiful love,
  Passionate and sublime,

And in one final act of peace,

They put an end,

To this sordid,

Rotten rhyme.

To wake in the arms of a lover

The call of a wild heart,
  As the night's cold permeates,
  While you, sadness, hope to thwart.

It morphs and moves,
  Evading every strike,
  Hoping that you'll fall.

Wishing to feast on your soul,
  As it jeers sinisterly,
  For in your pain, does it find its enthral.

A fight filled with heavy pant,
  As you shake your head violently,
  Wishing that she shall her painful words recant.

Why must sadness,
  Such a painful lover be?

Why must she tear my flesh from bone?

Why must she be,
The harbinger of pain and melancholy?

I love her so,
She gives my words,
The emotion which I hope to condone.

But my back to her,
I dare not turn,
For her evil intent does she wish to confer.

On a sullen poet's heart,
As he tries to keep his world together,
Before it inevitably falls apart.

But there she is,
The woman of scorn,
Who in sordid joy lightens her heart.

She caresses my heart with bony finger,
As she stokes the fires of my fear,
She watches the flames rise, appending evil tinder.

I have devoted myself to her,
But still, I wince at her touch,
As my heart is ultimately left in cinder.

As her haunting words,
To the imagination,
Don't leave much.

But still, I love her,
  Not out of love,
  But out of fear.

For another woman to take,
  Shall my heart,
  Finally, be resigned to a rotten fate.

And in a cold touch,
  Will my heart give in,
  To her heartless leer.

Of a lonely evening filled with fright,
  As the shadows of death,
  Fill my heart with hopeless delight.

As I lose myself to pure horror,
  While my stance is void of fight,
  And sordid laughter be found behind every corner.

In the absence of love,
  Am I left with nowhere to Hyde,
  As my heart calls for a lover to the heavens above.

With the strength of a tide,
  I call for love,
  And she cometh quickly.

Not on the wings of a dove,
  Or one which is filled with beauty,
  But in the tone of the sad and the sickly.

Yet still, I love the sordid lady fair,
For what else can a man do but love?
Lest his lonely heart be left bare.

So this I do pledge,
To a woman I haven't met,
And in loud cry do I her heart at peace set.

For fate has, into our story crept,
And in a hopeless tone,
The tide of fate has finally set.

The way in which our hearts,
Shall in hopeless embrace,
Be met.

Until then,
Bide your time my love,
For one day shall sadness be free.

Of lovers such as you and me,

And one day shall we be wed,
As my eyes will be wet,
With tears of melancholy.

As I finally shall be free,
From sadness, the woman,
Who has added to my misery.

And we shall in each other's arms find,

The treasures of the universe,
As we on each other's hearts dine.

And a morning sun will never cease,

As our hearts shall finally know peace.

For up until now,
Have they known nought but sorrow,
But now in a woman's arms,

Can my heart rejoice.
As with bated breath,
I open my eyes to your elegant beauty,

Tomorrow.

Once more in a lover's embrace to find,
The true love which will surely be mine.

And once more to find my heart,
In hopeful rhyme,

As in the arms of a lover,
Do I wake to find.

The powerful, the poetic and the sublime.

As we caress each other,

Lost in the gaze of the other,

For now and for all time.

The last man

The day of reckoning has come,
  In a moment of weakness have they been lost,
  To the power of an immortal son.

The corpses line the floor,
  As the mothers with cradled child,
  Try in vain to lock their doors.

With hopeless screech which fills the night,
  As the lifeless shadows are tilled,
  By holy, immortal light.

Wielded by the sons of gods,
  Who in hopeful songs,
  Open the gates and release the floods.

The hopeless die,
  The weak ones contorted,
  And the small ones cry.

As the devils and angels fight,

Once more another battle,
Once more a fight that will span across all time.

And in one fell swoop is the earth silent,
As one man stands alone,
With a smile does he stand defiant.

For gods sons have left,
The devils have been killed,
And this hopeless man, unkempt.

Sees the world alone,
For the masses,
Away have crept.

In the arms of the godly ones they fly,
As they escape the earth,
With hopeful smile, knowing they shall cease to cry.

Knowing in their hearts,
That they shall never again wince and wail,
That forevermore shall they never die.

Alone am I on this earth,
The one defiant man,
For he has chosen his sordid mirth.

Defiantly has he chosen to stand,
Before the wars of heaven,
Before the holy and the damned.

As he chooses to keep wearing his suit,
As elegantly, he clasps his hands.
With a façade of defiance does he stand.

He hopes for some control.
So he denies his hopeless soul,
Of those whom love, shall ultimately behold.

He plays a dangerous game of choice,
As a cup of tea, he does drink,
Suddenly he is confronted by holy voice.

'I love you good sir' she says,
In a voice full of sadness,
With eyes void of dread.

'Come and you shall see'
'The land you deny is hopeful and free'
'Of worry, sadness and melancholy'

He hears her voice and grunts,
For in hopeless jest,
Joy, does he hope not to confront.

With a gentle smile does an apparition appear,
A holy woman,
Whose eyes are strewn with tear.

Amazed and wordlessly he falls to his knees,
For the beautiful woman,
Through his façade does see.

Wordlessly she smiles,
  And looks at him with love,
  Adoration and a hint of tease.

As he a man, broken and defiled.
  With prayers before her feet,
  Can only beg for mercy from the heavens above.

'Fear not my love, and neither be scared',
  Does she in a beautiful voice confide.
  As her words descend on the back of a dove.

'For your love, have I chosen to leave,
  The hopeful land of life and light,
  The land of beauty and eternal reprieve'

With a worried frown do I look upon her,
  As her light vanishes,
  And all the holiness disappears from around her.

Before me now does a woman stand,
  With red dress and a glass of tea,
  Such a sight could I almost not withstand.

'Why must you leave that land?
  Why have you given up heaven for a man?'
  Say I softly as I try to stand.

Wordlessly am I found in an embrace,
  As I melt in her arms,
  As I finally, love can face.

And in a beautiful womanly tone,
Does she whisper to my heart,
As she hopes for some peace to condone.

This message of hers,
Was when I from my sadness had part.
As my knees from under me had given way,
As I quickly surrendered my heart.

For I was tired,
And though she a woman was,
Could I not help but her soul to admire.

For she had seen through my Façade.
And with a smile, I embraced her tight,
As her beautiful voice melted away my blight.

'A man have I chosen, my love,
You, that man may be,
So let's promise never to part.'

'For now and forevermore,

Let's dance on this earth,

And fear not for your lonely heart

For in hopeful wordless dance,
Will this silly woman bring your heart some mirth,
And with smiles and enthral will we be reborn'

In my arms will you find your heart,
  As with a gentle caress across your face,
  Shall I shake your resolve to the floor.

So how about that dance handsome sir?'

We're the only ones here after all'

In the dark, do they cower

The beauty of a dame,
So natural and wild,
One who hopes never to be tame.

One whose rose-kissed cheeks,
Has the resolve of the hooded ones,
All but defiled.

She springs across the fields,
In hopeful delight,
As the darkness cowers in unholy plight.

With a tender caress does she, hope confer,
As the tendrils of evil wince,
With a wail, they wish not for her anger to stir.

She throws herself upon a soft bed of flower,
Looking towards the sky in whisper,
With a breath do the evil ones cower.

A beautiful lady fair,

Whom to life and love,
Could not even in beauty, compare.

She, in a pure summer dress does sing,
As a delicate hand outstretched,
Vanquishes the beings of sin.

She looks with furrowed brow,
As the wilderness is void,
As her gladness is all but a whim.

An empty field of flower,
Void of life,
The shadows wincing as they cower.

With nary a man,
In warm embrace,
To make her his wife.

She sits bored and amused,
As the emptiness of this field,
Contrasts the shadows who are beaten and abused.

By the very sight of this pure maiden fair,
Who mortal fear in the evil ones, did muse,

For their worry at the sight of her,
To the fear of cosmic death,
Could not compare.

And yet she sits bemused,

In the absence of life,
Which this field does ruse.

They cower in terror,
At the thought of her flowing hair,
As the devils clad themselves in mortar.

As they are mortally terrified,
Of the delicate,
Beautiful lady fair.

Rose kissed lips and excitable skip,
Do the shadows hope never to find,
In an unholy trip.

To the land of the dead,
As they this field must pass,
As her beauty, this way had went.

And still, she sits with a womanly yawn,
As her eyes are filled with natural wonder,
When she finally can gaze at a natural fawn.

And she lay on a bed of flower,
In a field of light,
Surrounded by unholy hour.

For beyond her sight,
Lives the land of strife.

The land of death and entice,

The land which would take a poor man's life.
  The land which would destroy a woman,
  In a hopeless, mortal fight.

Yet still, she's alone,
  In the light which is her own.

So beautiful and free,

As she fills the devils with melancholy,

With a holy light,

Which permeates that eternal night.

And forever shall she be,

Beautiful elegant, wild, natural and free,

A beauty which rids the rotten souls,

Of their sordid,

Bighting,

Seething

Melancholy.

Eternal thirst

In hopeless prose,
Your life, void of mirth,
Comes to a sordid close.

And when I sleep,
Do the voices beckon thus,
Because they feel the call of thirst within all of us.

To be powerful and free,
"Away with the wanderlust!"
As the dead ones cause a hopeless fuss.

The living hearken not,
For how can they understand,
The pain of the dead one's lot?

So, they prod, poke and steal,
And hope with bated breath,
That the dead can no longer feel.

Any worry or pain,

For the living are too quickly slain,
And the graves all too quickly filled with names.

Of the innocent and pure,
Who in hopeless laugh jest,
For the living ones never pass the dead one's test.

When power of the 'other' is provided,
And in a blinding light,
Will two worlds have collided.

Beg not for the honorary and the well-confided.

For they shall die first,
And in hopelessness,
Will they forever thirst.

"More power for the powerful!
More power for the weak!
That's what you want!

That is what you truly seek!"

But little did they think,
That between melancholy and dream,
The most horrific of nightmare.

Is not easily seen,

For in the line between shadow and light,
Could you be struck with maddened sight.

And once more,

You will seek,

For power again,
  As the dead ones call for a friend.

As you,

Another shadow to the void,

Will ultimately append.

And wandering through a valley of shadow and death,

Shall your hoarse-filled thirst,

Never to come to a sordid end.

The prayer

Of an unholy hope,
   Do the masses pray,
   As they a sordid fire do Stoke.

With death and decay,
   Do the praying ones pray,
   And not a finger do they lift.

For to act, is not the Lord's way,
   With languages so beautiful and sweet,
   They beckon the weary and the meek.

To pray before idols of wood,
   To pray with money,
   As they stalk your neighbourhoods.

As they cackle amongst shadows of were,
   And speak evils to the guilty and bare.

They take the gold from an old man's hand,
   As they strike his knees with a club,

In hopeless cry, he finds himself unable to stand.

Still, he prays as they all do,
Not to a Lord,
But to the end of the morning dew.

For have you not heard?
Has it not been Said?
No more shall they pray to a Lord.

There is no hope to see in the way,
For the gods have brought death and decay.

But still, they pray,
Not to a Lord,
But the inevitable decay.

As the shadows give their holy words,
And the devils with cloak and hood,
Stalk the world.

With a hopeless shout, they cry out,
For nothing is clear,
As nothing will ever be found out.

And once more they pray,
Not to a Lord,
But to death and decay.

So, pray you,
Heed my words,

And take not kindly to clouds and birds,
  Hate the world,
  And hate your life.

For the ones that pray,
  Beckon only strife,
  And sordid decay is now their god.

As once more they poke and prod.

At the soul of a man,

Who is now their god.

Once more they pray,
  No more to devils and gods,

But forevermore,

To death and decay.

The beautiful lady fair

What more from a hopeful love to glean?
Of a beautiful lady fair,
Who caresses my dreams.

With a wonderful yellow dress,
Does she look at me with playful eyes,
As she, my cheek does gently caress.

Her rose-kissed cheeks so beautiful and free,
For a moment rids my heart,
Of sordid, seething melancholy.

A beautiful lady fair,
Preciously holding my head,
Natural as a wild mare.

Who all sadness from my heart,
With a soothing voice,
Abolishes with care.

She is now my heart,
For in her arms,
Could I a lifetime depart.

She is now my eyes,
For now through her beautiful eyes,
Do I lose all mortal ties.

With her gentle hand in mine,
Do I forgo my life,
As I live by her side for all time.

As she whispers in my ear,
Sweet nothings,
Which bring me to joyous tear.

For though beautiful and natural is she,
We both find happiness,

As we share hopelessly,
In our loving melancholy.

Hand in hand,
With a heart so free,
As together we stand,

Both broken pieces of a single person,
As I hope for this life,
Still to understand.

But wanting am I left,

As a lifetime of pious joy,
Do I wish to bet.

On beautiful,
Kind,
Loving eyes.

Which many an hour have wept,
Which my knees from under me,
With the batting of an eyelash have swept.

I'm enamoured by her,
Her womanly love,
Through whom all sadness from me is kept,

As she stands with outstretched arm,
So my wandering eyes,
Can see no alarm.

She is one with all,
And fills my heart,
With beautiful enthral.

So once more my dear,
Rid my melancholic heart,
Of sordid, terrible fear,

And give me that beautiful,

Womanly leer.

As I pledge with a mind so clear,

To rid your enchanting eyes,

Of all your tears.

As hand in hand,
  Heart in heart,

We live on for all time,

Year after year.

And once more a morn to hear you say.

‘Good morning, my handsome dear

How about a day of wonderful joy and worship,
  Filled with mirth and enthral.

As we love each other in good cheer?’

Now come on you melancholic soul,

You’re my greatest friend after all,

Let’s frolic for all time,

And dance forevermore’

As a lover dies

In hopeless prance,
  Do the suited and dressed ones,
  Waltz and dance.

To an immortal song of woe,
  As the men and woman are locked in a hopeful trance,
  With music played by magical bones,

Who tap their skeletal feet in delight.

As the men and women dance wordlessly,
  And into each other's eyes,
  Do they find the absence of the evil night.

As one more man looks up to see,
  The Deathly band,
  And in a swift movement is freed.

From hopeful dance,
  The shadows take him away,
  For he dared to commit a hopeless deed,

For, in the eyes of the dead,
  Has the lost young man moved beyond rebuttal,
  For he has learnt the absence of glee.

As a woman suddenly sees,
  The dead ones scuttle,
  Along the floor and between their knees.

Searching for one more to take,
  For they dared to look from their lover's eyes,
  In a Waltz that transcends fate.

They danced and dance,
  To the music of the 'other',
  They never hope from their lover's eyes to glance.

For in a moment would they be lost,
  To the land of nothing,
  To the land of eternal frost.

As the bony vaudeville sings,
  And the devils serve you tea,
  Encouraged by the hooded ones sins.

In this ball of evil and delight,
  Which never has seen,
  The delicate touch of Holy light.

Forevermore they dance,
  Hoping not from their lover,
  Ever to glance.

For if they in weakness may lose sight,
  Of their lover's tear-filled eyes,

In a moment will they dance no more,

As their body shall hit the marble floor.

And their lover will cry an immortal cry.

For their lover has finally died.

And once more the others will dance,
  Hopelessly they shall prance,
  Only in their lover's embrace to confide,

For the lovers mourning cry,
  Filled with mortal shriek,
  Shakes the other dancers to the core,

Yet still,
  Hand in hand,

They shall gaze into each other's eyes,

As they dance forevermore.

The woman of scorn

The readers read forevermore,
  As the living and the hopeful,
  Line the rotting floor.

With hope and sordid song,
  They want for a world,
  Void of sadness and wrong.

A hopeless foray,
  Guided by suits and smiles,
  With their ungodly charade.

With promises and ideas,
  Do they put an end,
  To even the wisest of fears.

They sneer in delight,
  As the hope they bestow,
  Saves someone from their rotten plight.

But haven't you heard?

Is sadness not as much human?
Should melancholy not also be heard?

Why must we hate her so?
What has she done?
But brought truth and death in tow.

She winces at our jest,
She hides from our laughter,
For it hurts her, this can her heart to attest

Will nobody love her?
Will she walk forevermore?
Barefoot and scorned?

For she was born,
Of the sordid valley of thorn.

She knows nothing but truth,
And she cannot understand the whims,
Of the suited ones scorn.

They promise the unholy mass,
That they shall murder in cold blood,
This fair, delicate lass.

For her words beckon truth,
And to this end, does the world,
Call her evil, ill-begotten and crass.

With a look of dread, she runs,

Further and further, she runs.

As the masses chase,
With pitchfork and firelight,
As the masses call to have their fun.

With the woman of scorn and hate,
Who in hopeless run through the woods,
Hopes to escape her final fate.

At the hands of the learned ones,
She will her last days spend,
In the stocks of pain.

So too will the simple ones,
Their love for her disdain.
Forever satiate as they dress her cloak with bloody stain.

And once more she shall call out,
Not speaking the lies of the suited ones,
But the truth of fate.

In hopeful grin, they'll keep her alive,
As to break her body and spirit,
Will the suited ones with evil grin strive.

And once more will she die,
Hopelessly in a grand display,

Will the suited ones take her life,

To once more be born in the valley of thorns.

And search forevermore.

For a kind voice to hear,
  For a hopeless lover to shed a tear.

At her eternal plight,

As her stories of hopeless misery,

Are relegated to whispers of the night.

One more sordid deadline

The glory of a thousand love stories,
  Lost to an age of reason,
  Lost to an age of worry.

As the work of a thousand,
  Doesn't hope in one's life
  -Ultimately land.

As the spirit of a single life,
  Very quickly waxes and wanes,
  But ultimately still slips away like falling sand.

Through the fingers of the earnest,
  The saddened ones,
  And the free.

Do the hearts of the hard-working,
  And the early ones
  -Fill with cynical sadness and atrocity.

No end to the crack of a taskmaster's whip,

As a woman in high heels climbs a hill,
With straw strewn back and meaningless whit.

No time to spend worthlessly,
As the husks of human flesh,
All to a moving metal tin do cling earnestly.

For the men and women are no longer alive,
And though to iron gods and metal heavens,
Do they ultimately strive.

The work of a thousand slaves has never left one alive,

For ultimately another must finally die.

So that the taskmasters may ultimately thrive.

On the dreams of the saddened,
The honest,
And the wise.

Do the dead ones lead the drive,
At the helm of nature's lies,
Do they the unholy train ultimately ride.

One with a single passenger who in jest,
Grins at their arrival,
For he is not one of the men and women who've died.

Nay, he is the only one who is truly alive,

For he, on their work and soul,

Does ultimately thrive.

And with a jester's smile does he say to their sullen soul,

The once truth but ultimate lie,

"Well done young soul,
  But don't forget,

Your folly, in a thousand more hours,
  Does ultimately lie,

So, wake up once more for me will you?
  For you have a thousand more hours of work,
  Before you can ultimately die,

So, beg, plead and writhe,

But don't forget your management of time,
  Nor to drown your fear in misery and wine,

For if you fail me,

Shall the wrath of the universe be ultimately divine,

So, work once more,
  For your husk of a soul.

Will always be the taskmaster's ultimate dine,

And your once sordid, worthless life,

Is ultimately mine,

So, chop chop,

This train isn't yet at the end of the line,

You still have one more sordid deadline."

The fool who dares

Restlessly I stir in my bed,
As fear and torment grip my heart,
As the shadows play a sickly game in my head,

A movement in the dark,
As the shadows are so clear to me,
For their form is simple and stark.

I turn to see nothing there,
Not a thing,
Standing before me.

But I could have sworn,
That the creatures were there,
The creatures of evil and scorn.

Which madness around their eyes,
In sordid, evil brightness,
Have adorned.

What more can I say?

For nothing is there,
So again I lay down my head,

As I stir and beg,
That once more comfort will come to me,
That once in my life I may enjoy my bed.

And again, the shadows prevail,
With sordid screech,
They wince and they wail.

For they wish to be known,
Their evil wishes to prevail,
They thirst for my final act of fail.

They watch and plea,
To the gods of the sun and the sea,
As they shuffle, broken and frail.

Only their madness to adorn,
For they speak in tongues,
And again they wince and wail.

If only for a moment had I listened closely to their wails,
Would I have saved my soul,
From eternal, evil sail.

For in a shivering whisper do they speak,
Of terrors that haunt the meek,

The stupid sordid meek,

Who into that evil abyss,

Had dared to peak.

So once more shall I beg,
For a cosy, homely bed.

But little did I know,

That my soul is already dead.

And the shadows will haunt me forevermore,

Not to haunt, but to warn.

Never again to dip a toe in the evil spring.

And never to engage in that final, sordid sin.

And again, like every other,
I will not hearken,
To the souls who have died.

For they are scary and ugly,
And in their council do I hope,
Never again to confide.

The unholy bog

This end of a scientist,
   Is my final Ill begotten warning,
   To all those who thirst,

To all those who dare to trod,
   Beyond the mist of that,
   Evil, ghostly bog,

Riddled with mist and intrigue,
   Did the music from beyond,
   Fill my heart with such joy,

That my weary legs,
   With wonder and hope,
   Could travel many a league.

As I beyond a grove had crept,
   Did I come to a ball of wonder,
   And admittedly,

The sight of beautiful ladies' fair,

Did I find quite immense.

As the well-dressed vaudeville sang a wondrous song,
While suited men and beautiful women,
Appeared joyously dancing and prancing in beautiful throng.

But Foolish was I not to see,
In between the beautiful dames,
Behind the darkened trees,

Evil,
Seething,
Writhing,
Shadow.

Is all from my corpus of the English language,
That my mind can condone,

For beyond the edge of that clearing lined with tree,

Was something inexplicably,

Staring back at me,

Not the eyes of a man,
Nor the eyes of a god,

But the eyes of evil,
The evil who has brought upon my mind,
Many a thought of sod.

For he, or she or it... I cannot tell,

Are not hallowed,
  As they on this land have befallen.
  Screeching with wondrous joys to sell.

Fallen from the heavenlies,
  Is all I wish to say,

But again, I'm sure you won't believe me at the end of the day.

A scientist am I,

But still, I ran,

For the eyes of that creature wasn't a man's.

Nor a woman,

Nor a beast,

No, the eyes of that creature,

Would surely on my soul,

Have made an unholy feast.

A couple, in love

The love of a woman of beauty,
So wonderful,
Full of the essence of nature and glee.

Wonderfully Wondrous,
Captivating and free,
But not free of sordid melancholy,

Not free of that infernal yoke,
Strapped to everyone's back,
As the evil ones jest and joke.

They watch us from up above,
As they in malevolent tone,
Hope to question our love.

But still, she stands strong,
The love of my life,
Flawed but void of wrong.

Delicate like broken glass,

And just as sharp,

Slender fingers which,
With womanly elegance,
Can strike my heart like a harp.

A tightly strung harp,
Which many a hope in life,
Has found the soul to part.

Yet still, together we stand,
Soul in soul,
Hand in hand.

As we forevermore gaze upon the stars,

A beautiful Woman and a sullen man.

And once more she will say,
At the beautiful end of that day.

"Come my love,
Let's find our way,

Lest we in this horrid valley,
Will have to stay."

And once more with hopeful glance will I my heart,
To my eternal lover parlay.

As I in a whisper,

To her do say.

"Very well my love,
Let us not tarry long.

The heavenlies await,
And so too does the satiating fruit,

Of our chaotic,

Blissful, eternal fate,"

The dichotomy of love

The way of the hopeless lover,
 Is strewn with corpse and despair,

With a staggered stumble,
 She walks towards a light unknown,
 A voice so sweet struck with mumble.

Of a strange magic which her heart,
 Had taken hold,
 A magic which from horror does seldom part.

She wishes for a lover,
 She wishes for a king,
 She hopes to love him forever.

A man is one of many on this earth,
 But he would surely bring,
 With a neat suit and a smile some sordid mirth.

A man begs for home,
 As he rides a train towards the west,

Reading the passing scenery like a sacred tome.

The words of nature beckon to his heart,
With sordid misery does she beg,
For a lover, for one who will have her heart.

The young man smiles as he sees,
Nature,
And her whinging misery.

For he knows her essence well,
Is not the heart of this man filled with melancholy?
Is this not the nature of his eternal well?

Filled with black ink as he writes in earnest,
The dreams he adores,
The ones from which reality is furthest?

In a sordid twist of fate,
Do these two meet,
In passing walk are each other's gaze met.

As the eyes of the other could not for an eternity,
Such instant love ever hope,
To satiate.

A hopeless lover and a scholar,
Meet with bated breath,

A woman in love with an apparition,
And a man who writes of a beautiful ghost.

They smile,
  Once more as they embrace.

Not in the dreams they love,
  Nor in some strange magical fate,

A choice do they make,
  A lover and a scholar,

As they kill their dreams,

For true love,

With terrible,

Hopeless smile.

Have they finally seen.

And they kiss,
  And they dance,
  And they love forevermore.

For their dreams of love,
  Have they killed,
  And the entrails have they strewn across the floor.

And in one beautiful,

Hopeful,

Glee-filled kiss.

Do they finally realise this.

An apparition can only love so much,
A ghost can never feel your touch.

The love of the dead,

Can only ever fill with dread.

So love away young lovers!

Though he not a king,
And her heart strewn with sin.

They embrace and kiss once more,

Though void of fairytale magic,

Hand in hand they frolic,

In a world of despair,

Locked in each other's,

Love-filled gaze,

Forevermore.

The unholy track

Of an end do I hope,
One which will validate the fare,
Of this iron train which bellows smoke.

Unholy smoke flowing endlessly,
As this infernal train moves,
From land to land, hopelessly.

Almost wandering like a man cluelessly,
Had I considered such a fact,
Would I have known that this train is eternal.

And lest I had jumped out a long time ago,
I am bound to the metal frame,
My own soul must I now forgo.

For this train shall follow forevermore,
The tracks strewn by death and destiny,
As we pass the sordid moors.

As we pass scenery void of life,

In a train built on melancholy,
Misery, and strife.

Lest you misunderstand, this train has no conductor,
Nor crew,
Nor any semblance of hopeful instructor.

For death's train seldom runs in the day,
And eternal night plunges my heart into love's foray.

The empty halls call for companionship,
The echoed, hoarse calls,
Every semblance of hope from my heart does strip.

Oh, silly me,
Why couldn't I see?

The void of a train's cabin is far from free,
Of others who can end my loneliness,
Of those who can satiate my melancholy.

Yes, I am not alone in this infernal train,
Bound to the tracks which lead to the end,
Filled with nought but unholy pain.

Nay, surrounded am I by wondrous beings,
With shapes so strange and wonderful,
With hearts that have surely stopped beating.

Yes, surrounded am I by dead ones,
As we talk and consider,

Which cosmic jester, this train funds.

We laugh and drink and make merry,
As another cigarette is smoked,
As we open another bottle of Sherry.

For the train will always move regardless,

Never stopping,

Never ceasing,

As our infernal end,
Is to forever wander the abyss.

Making merry,
As we open another bottle of Sherry.

And once more I'll awake,

In a moving train,
As my heart is once more,
Strewn with pain.

Oh, silly me I forgot to say,
The dead ones visit and delay my pain,
Only for a single day.

And when they leave,
Does my heart wince,
For I must prepare my soul.

For aeons alone,

In this infernal train,
Which beckons for the end of life,
Which sings odes to hopeless mortal pain.

That I have to satisfy,
For my life was nought,
But a musical Waltz with myself and I.

So alone do I this train ride,
For all time,
As I scour the abyss far and wide.

Searching for an end,
Or at least some hope upon this sordid heart,
To finally append.

But wanting am I found,
As the train moves steadily,
On the tracks laid out on the ground.

Not by sadness or melancholy,
But the sordid tracks I built,
When I was young and free.

I lied dear reader, for there is a captain to this ship,
And he is the sordid man,
Who built the tracks to this unholy trip.

The man who rides this train,

Was the composer of the musical piece,
To which the chugging beat mirrors a heart of pain,

And once more I shall confide,
In nobody and nothing,
As my eternal train shall I ride.

Towards a forever, filled with nothing,
Searching forever for a semblance of something.

And once more this sordid man will cling,
To a train, he built with his own hands,
The train built of sin.

Dancing and prancing in sordid blight,
For outside is void of any hopeful light.

And once more a song for the flesh of a dead man,
As once more I look out the window,
A dead man who in pride does stand.

Forever to ride this ill-begotten train,

Forever to wish for a living lovcr,

Forever, on the train, which clings,

To Melancholic,

Evil,

Unholy Tracks.

The strange man in jesters' clothes

My heart overflows,
  Black ink,
  Scratching away at white paper.

My heart do I wish to bestow,
  Upon a sordid page,
  Stark, clinical and which to nothing, is prone.

The words escape my lips,
  In a great outpouring of nothing,
  Do I, in my own mind sit.

Writing and writing and writing,

Of that which is,
  Naught but this.

'A word for a feeling!' Cry, the weak,
  'The sad end of a miserable life!'
  Say the unholy meek.

And what say you?
  The readers,
  The one whose mind I seek?

I am one who wishes to live forevermore,
  So, in hopeless jest, I write,
  On the ceilings, the windows and the floors.

Hoping to catch your eye,
  Yes you, the reader!
  Do I wish in your mind to confide.

My misery and thought,
  Of which words are bellowing,
  And with the truth are fraught.

Oh, but don't listen to silly ol' me,
  All I write of is rooted in sordid melancholy.

But again, I must ask,
  What more of it?
  What more, is of my mortal task?

So, in prose, I question thus,
  The terror in all of us.

And I am shocked and flabbergasted to see,
  That none of us are truly free.

Yes, you!
  The reader too!

You aren't free,

Of the tendrils of evil,
  Of sordid sadness and glee.

The universe plays a lovely tune,
  And in our hearts do we feel the runes,
  Beckon and ebb and flow.

As she beckons our hearts,
  To never let go.

Of that which we should hold dear,
  And make sure you never show your fear.

Yes, you dear reader!

Never show your fear.

Because the attention of that which is unknown,
  You must never hope to leer.

Or your gaze a little longer in the abyss to ever peer.

Yes, you the reader!
  I write this warning once more.

Never trust a suited leader,
  Or the whims of those who mourn.

For shadows revel in the absence of light,

So too in your misery,
Do they find their delight.

Hopelessly wandering, the evil things,
Hoping to break your soul,
By ripping it, at the seams.

Oh my, I may have said too much,
My life is on the line,
A line void of such.

The embrace of a lover's touch,
And the beautiful song,
Of the one, I may love too much.

So, I say again dear reader,
Or I, in jest do ask.

That you, hold onto this immortal task,
Don't forget my rhyme and prose.

For this is the poetry of a strange man,

A strange man in jester's clothes

They cry

An image of a woman crosses my mind,
With hands in mine,
Do our hearts appear intertwined.

We sing and hope and love,
As we look to the night sky for comfort.
As together do we worship the stars above.

For together they stay,
Never waxing,
Never waning.

Only ever coming for a time,
And leaving for the morning,
Without complaining.

Of sadness and melancholy,
Of riches or poverty,
The skies beg not for glee.

Or in hopeless prose,

To finally feel free,
Of the cold grasp of death and decay.

Nor the sins of the holy and meek.

A strange thought enters my mind,
Though small and insignificant,
The thought of life starts out sublime.

A hopeless laugh escapes my lips,
As I hold my head in my hands,
As the adrenaline of misery, rattles my fingertips.

Suddenly am I in an embrace,
As she shivers in sync with me,
As a hopeless smile on her lips, do trace.

As she looks into my eyes with love,
The natural love of an angel,
Void of mirth and want.

But still a lover,
Still a beautiful woman.
Who doesn't upend a front.

As hopelessly she cries too,
And heart in heart,
Do we from our stoic smiles part.

And in an act of true love,
Do we cry and wince and wail,

We mourn the death of the ones above.

We mourn the ages lost,
We mourn each other's eternal cost.

And though someday I shall die,
At least this day in my lover's arms,
Could I cry.

Void of happiness and mirth,
But still in each other's arms,
To share the hurt.

For she waits for both us,
My lover and I,

To take our souls,
From this sordid life.

And though a worrisome prospect this may be,
Our tears can still be dried by each other,
As we share in hopeless melancholy.

But for today,
Shall we in each other's arms cry.

For someday,

Will the light be taken away,

The breath shall leave our lungs,

The life shall depart from our eye,

But until that sordid day arrives,

Shall we, in one another's,
  Warm embrace,

Wince,

And wail,

And cry.

A poet in chains

My love holds my heart in a vice,
  Black ink trails from it,
  As it's squeezed tight.

Every time your gaze meets mine,
  Or In a waltz of fate,
  I am met with your wondrous sight.

Of elegance and beauty,
  At which my heart enthrals,
  As it yearns for your childish tease.

I walk away happily,
  Void of sadness,
  Filled with glee.

For a great wonder of creation, you are,
  And though I search near and far,
  Bemused am I to find the absence of your beautiful heart.

I cannot describe what pulls me to you,

I'm simply enraptured,
And to this end are my words true.

They speak of a madman,
Who shivers as he writes,
For his cold heart is in want of one who will understand.

One who will finally care,
One who a moment of their time,
Will hope to spare.

To speak to my heart,
To hug me tightly,
To wish never from my arms to part.

What more could I hope to see?
But a sordid morning,
Void of sadness and melancholy.

What more is there from this universe to glean?
But hopeless mirth,
In a poetic prance with glee.

Beg for this ending, I shall,
As I bide my heart,
As I have committed to love you with enthral.

And now and forevermore does my heart flutter,
As I, beautiful words to myself do mutter.

Hoping that you'll hear,

As your beautiful laugh,
And wondrous beauty.

Does, drive away every worry,
And every fear.

And to this end do I thirst for you,
As a man in a deserty abyss,
I thirst for a lover who is true.

And once more I will sing,
A song of melancholy,
Soaked in sin.

For a poet am I,
And to this end do I ultimately write.

To have my innards strewn on paper,
The creases of my heart surgically cut,
And my innermost secrets given to the masses, without waver.

And still a hopeless romantic am I,
As I try to say 3 simple words, for all time.
"I love you", was that so hard to say outside of rhyme?

Well in any case,

It matters not for long.

For my heart will forever admire your beauty.

Not from afar though,

But from your loving arms.

Someday...

Someday I say,

That I, my loving heart to you,

Will ultimately parlay.

But until then, let me see your eyes once more,

As my resolve is cast to the cold floor.

And in hopeless mirth, will I worship,

The beauty you have refined in your lifelong hardship.

And once more I'll write and sing,
  In melancholy and sin.

As I gaze into your heart,
  Like the depths of an ocean from which I hope,
  Never to part.

So once more my dear,

Could you give me one more womanly leer?

Perhaps an elegant laugh,

Or an emotional tear?

Because all are hallowed to me,

And the very sight of you,

Gives my heart some glee.

Fill my soul with everything but melancholy.

Give this prisoner of love, a chance,

To feel what it feels like,

In absence of law,
To truly feel free.

A beautiful dame for all eternity

Is there a place in the heart for true love?
Or in absence of truth,
Does the heart wish from joy to part?

What is the mirth of a joyous glance?
Without the beautiful dame,
Accompanied by a wondrous chance.

At love and loving forevermore,
Wondrous, lovely, feelings of joy,
As we lay a blanket on the grassy floor.

Your head on my lap,
As my heart have, I laid,
In your womanly trap.

One which, with bated breath,
Do I hope never to escape from,
As your loving eyes, void of harm

Bring my heart to peace,

In your loving, tender,
Slender arms.

And once more you will ask,
'My love... My love, wish you, from this mortal realm to part?'

And again, I shall my love, with a kiss impart.

As I, to you shall say.

"Now darling, of the thought of the end of this day,
Does my heart break apart.

Now my dear, give me a womanly leer,

Lest I, in madness shall reel,
And the prospect of the absence of your warmth,
Fill me with fear."

And once more you chuckle and leer,
As you end all my fears,
And to my heart do say.

'My love, fear you not for the end of the day,

For this shall I,

To your heart say,

There is no one else for whom,
I shall my delicate heart,

Parlay.

Except the man, in whose arms I wish to lay.
Now stay your tongue, you silly fool, of a lovestruck man,

Kiss me deeply and don't fret your head,
My love, need you not covet.
You would do well if you, this, would understand.

For I am yours and you are mine,

And so too, shall we be intertwined,

As we kiss,

And love and dine,

On each other's hearts,

For all time'

Smile forevermore

Smile young child,
  Never cry,
  Lest you shall your parents' defile.

Yes, isn't it so wonderful to, see?
  A beautiful nursery filled,
  With happiness and mirth as far as the eye can see?

Oh yes, now young man you better not cry,
  Lest the shadows shall hear of this,
  And you may be forced to lie.

Oh dear,
  Oh me,

A slip of the tongue,
  And some sordid melancholy.
  For this, do you have my apologies.

Yes, now once again smile young lady fair,
  For the end is never near,

And your mirth is always found at the end of a nightmare.

Yes, smile one and all,
Smile and never tear,
For in sadness do the bad ones fall.

And we cannot, such silliness condone,
Mind you, we've tried,
We've always let the sad ones amongst us live.

But didn't you see what they did?
They spoke of horrid truth,
And even the sordid poor had they defended!

Oh! The travesty!
Oh! Even the Lord above,
Could never, to their ill-begotten souls, grant amnesty.

Yes! I tell you once more,

Cry not,

Shed not a tear,

For the heart is open to truth when you do,

And it's rather perturbing for me and you.

So, trust this suited friend of all,
I mean,
Would a suited one to you blatantly lie?

Can't you see how the sad ones,
In their sordid misery,
Could have led to our inevitable fall?

Surely you, wouldn't want the truth,
To have any chance in sordid enthral.

Think of the children I say!
For the children, should we,
Your truth parlay!

And have no fear,
You will live in great cheer.

In pencil box houses,
Sturdy in frame,
Built on the evil ones fear.

Who are the evil ones, you ask young one?

Hardly men and women I say.
Yes, more akin to sordid evil shadows,
Or evil in the night, at the end of a wonderful day.

Yes, young ones listen to me,
For in my handcuffs,
Will you find yourself truly free.

Of sordid sadness,
Worry,
And melancholy.

So once more I tell you,
  Cry not,
  Shed not a single tear,

For if you do,

Then this smiling,

Suited man,

Will be your greatest fear.

A stranger's hand to take

The darkness is void of light,
And so too,
Does the light beckon for the fight.

Between shadows and holy flame,
Which permeates,
The sordid, freezing, night.

Do you will for it?
Do you truly see yourself fit?

To engage in battles, millions of years old,
As the shadows beg for more war,
As the devils become more bold?

Oh, but don't tear young one,
Oh no, perish that thought,
For the world calls for happiness and fun.

Never have a nightmare about sordid evil,
For they exist in the mind,

And there do they roam.

Prancing and dancing,
Singing and whinging,
Beckoning for a friend,

And to this call should we never attend,
Oh, young one, never attend to their call.
For in their eyes lives deathly harm, in their arms, lives humanities fall.

Oh, and never listen to strangers,
Nor men in the night,
Cloaked with horror, plagued by delight.

All too, I suppose in time, you'll learn,
For now, hold my hand,
And let's leave the land that burns.

Ah! But I must warn, fear also the angel,
The angel which holds your hand,
For though workers of light are they.

Their appearance is rather strange, I'd say,
Clad in darkness lest they wake you in your sleep,
And always silent as they move, hoping not to wake the meek.

You see young one,
The spirit world is full of games, wonders and fun,

But dare you not,

To find the lot,

Of the beings which this land call home,
Lest you shall search your life,
For an evil tome.

To read, as you,
Your feet in the air do kick,
And be lost in a world of evil, on a sinful trip.

The spirit world is wondrously beautiful,
But look not beyond the shadow,
Seek not beyond the meadow, filled with birds and bees.

Walk not past the hallowed forest,
Nor past the trees and leaves.

For clad in darkness are they,
The ones who in sordid evil,
Plunge the souls of children into the eternal foray.

Their hauntingly clear eyes,
Discernible from their dark coats,
Clad in nothing but the voices of the lost.

Who adorns their naked evil,

And the screams of children,
Which fuel their lot.

Worse than Angel,

Worse than Devil,

And standing beyond the treeline,
With a jester's smile,

Does he pace back and forth,

Waiting for the next wandering child.

But take no heed to evil and horror young one,
Take my hand now,

Let's frolic over there,
Past the tents of light and sound.

And past the trees,
And the birds,
And the bees.

Let's go for a walk,
And have a little talk.

Oh, worry not for my horrific words,
Or my scary stories,
They are just that, stories, you need not worry.

Now let's go and see,

What freedom of choice truly means.

And beyond the holy lands do trod,

Into the accursed unholy bog.

And once more a child shall be lost,
As they take my hand,
And follow me into the eternal frost.

Oh, silly me,
I forgot about the reader here,
Oh, I'm sure you're rather confused by me.

Oh yes,
I'll let you,
For a little moment guess.

For I am not devil,
Nor angel, nor man,

I'm worse,
For I steal, I kill,
And I destroy lands.

But you also know me,
Don't you remember?

That time I took your hand too,
And taught you of the Ill begotten truth?

Behind the cloaked shadow,
In between the border of light and darkness,
The horror of mirth.

Oh, but fret not dear friend,
  Soon you'll see,

Someday soon,
  You may remember me,

The conjurer of dreams,
  So wonderful and sweet,

And always to drink on your tears,
  As you tremble helplessly.

Oh, I've said too much,

I'll be on my way now,

But don't you worry about evils such,

As the ones you can only dream of, in melancholy.

For there are far worse things,

Than devils, shadows and honesty.

And perhaps my name will you remember.

For I was the death of innocence,
  And alive do I writhe.

Beyond the shadow of death,

Beyond the sordid tide.

Of time, which on the backs of people,
  Doth ride.

And forevermore will I in the tears of children confide.

Now follow me young one,

The world of the adults is full of fun.

Dancing and prancing and never being down.

Except when death calls,

And even he will meet you with a reversed frown!

Now follow me.

And I shall show you what it's like to truly be free.

In sadness and misery,

In sordid, unholy melancholy.

In that which evil,

Wishes from this mortal realm,

Would finally be set free.

The lament of creation

What hope is there for those who've died?
  Can a dead man,
  In a woman's arms ever lie?

What of a sordid man?
  One who nary a person,
  Could their horrible gaze stand?

And what if I am not a man?
  Could a woman ever, my heart,
  Truly understand?

Mind you,
  I am a creation of man too.

But not merely of flesh and blood,
  Though I, mirth and joy can see,
  From melancholy am I rather free.

Except for one fact,
  For my creators,

Had chosen in unholy pact.

To make me yearn for love forevermore,
To only give me tear ducts,
So, I may cry on the floor.

Yet everything else,
Not a man, nor a beast.
Nor a monster who wishes on your heart to feast.

And still, I am bound.

In this eternal metal prison,
Would my sordid heart be found.

For I wait for a princess so fair,
Who to my terrible appearance,
May never, have a care.

Oh! My hatred for my human creators,
As high as my love for them.

They made me human,
Only in tears and fear of death.

Yet still am I perfect in every way,
My stiff mannerisms,
And the polite words I say.

But they know the truth,
The humans that made me,

That in honest cry, do I only wish to be loved freely.

But which woman can love a man,
If he no longer a man was?

Which woman would embrace me,
If all they can feel,
Is oily, fleshy misery?

I'm not a man,
Nor a beast,
Nor a monster.

But much is to be said for the soul,
Which only the Lord himself,
Could care to understand.

So, I wait,
With bated breath, I wait.

For my angel to come,
Whether she be a woman,
Or death which my soul, from its mortal coil,

Has wrung.

May she come,
For I will wait.

For love, forevermore,

Even In the face of stupid fate.

Because though flesh and metal am I,
  I really hope, never to have to die.

Without the embrace of a woman so fair,
  Without having to wake up from another sordid nightmare.

This thought makes me want to cry,
  For there is a chance that I might die.
  Or perhaps like the others.

When sight upon me do set,
  She might walk away with a sigh.
  For mine is the sight of wretch.

Hardly a face, or a wonderous voice,
  Was given to me by fate,

Instead, I have a heart.
  A stupid, poet's heart.
  A heart, which, with every clinical vice.

Wishes for a lady,
  Who may love me.
  A woman who will never wish, from me, to ever part.

So, in hopelessness, I wait,

For a princess someday,

Who can love my fate.

And my sordid tears in her shoulder,
  Allow to embrace with love,
  As my lonely heart, in pain,

For her wonderous beauty, did wait.

Finally when she, my soul's yearning.

With beautiful, womanly voice and sight.

In horrible dance with a monster,

Shall satiate.

The dark cell, I call my home

The cold drip of dew against steel,
   Drowns the heart in fear,
   As the caged one, which hopes to feel.

Something more than melancholy,
   Perhaps a bit less misery,

Imagine the image,
   Of a wonderful voyage,

Across the waters of evil,
   In a boat made of joy,
   And void of devil.

A cage in and of itself,
   But one that moves,
   Across the water's shelf.

Towards lands unknown,
   And living ones who also live alone.

But for now, I must gaze out,
Out of the metal bars,
That make up my hut.

Oh, not a hut of dirt and tar,
But a metal cage,
For which the outside is void of light both near and far.

And soft echoing sounds permeate the dark,
As my own hands before my face,
Could I hardly make out in the dim light so stark.

From the warmth of my dreams,
Which even to glimpse for a moment,
Bursts my heart at its seams.

And once more to wait,
Oh yes, I wait,
I know not how long; night and day are not part of this fate.

Only eternal dusk,
Well, I call it dusk,

But more akin to moonlight,
Permeating a dark forest.

As I look outside my prison cell,
Wondering, waiting,
Musing on the fate of those who fell.

With me into eternal night,

As the calls and wails of the beings outside,
Cause quite a fright.

You see, this cage is quite humorous,
For though dark, dank,
And very much not glamorous.

The cage is locked from the inside,
And forevermore will you do best to bide your time.

For empty cages fill this prison,
Unlocked from inside,
Patrolled by shadow, who with death, does confide.

For if you, a dangerous thing,
Such as freedom had sought.

Oh! Perish the thought, dear reader!
Perish the thought!

For such an end,
Could I not describe,
Without my stomach turning to knot.

And once more I muse again,
Of a wonderful beach,
And a pleasant lady-friend.

From the world, I try never to forget,
For many of the cages are empty,

And lest we forget,

The dark is never empty,
Simply filled by creature, of evil and regret.

Open the cage.

And perhaps will your mind at peace be set.

By the movement of that which cannot be seen,
And once more will my heart burst at the seams,

Not of gladness but of bloody melancholy.

So, I wait here and my time do I bide,
Lest my mind,
On a wonderful dove, were to ride.

Far away from my mortal coil,
As the end of all ages,
Is fraught with dripping oil.

Which in a moment would I light to see,
The shadowy eyes of the dark,
Forever staring back at me.

And once more will my hand caress,
The key to this prison cell,
As my resolve is put to the test.

And once more a day or a night to find,

A memory once more,

Of lady fair and love,

As I beg for the hours to fly by,

So again, I may take my rest.

Forevermore, to wait with bated breath,

Forever, in cold shivering brick walls to confide.

Forever, to dream a little less,

As in this cage, I call my home.

Do I live for all time,

Now and forevermore,

To wait

For the final end, to my ill-begotten rhyme.

Death's melancholy

In a moment do many die,
As the masses return from wars,
As the widowers finally cry,

The jesters sing and dance,
So too, in your melancholy do they,
Laugh and prance.

In suits made of gold and stars,
As they delight in the decay,
Both near and far.

A mother hates her child,
For in her hopeless mirth,
Doth the child only know, that which is absurd.

"My child must quickly grow,
Lest misery and torment,
Shall follow in tow."

But little did she know,

Little did she see,

The greatest of life's lies,
Is sealed in a neat bow,
In a suit, it speaks of misery.

Not a simple personified misery,
But death wearing a neat bow tie,
As his pestilence upon the damned does free.

With a bony smile, he watches,
As the living ones writhe and seethe,
He grimaces as the dead ones spread unholy melancholy.

Death winces at their breath,
The true dead ones,
Who in hopeful eyes, their ending have met.

"Say, Death,
Shall you come here a while?
Perhaps I need your help to attain this land of camomile"

Says a suited one,
Void of life in his eye,
In want of fun.

Death tries to withdraw,
But the smell of blood,
Seeps into his bony pores.

In an act of instinct, he lurches to the lands,

Of sand and tea,
He reaps the souls in one gentle cleave.

And he falls once more to his knees,
In sadness and in a bony heart rid of glee.

For again did the suited ones leer,
And once more will the living,
Death's presence, fear.

And though he may lend a helping hand,
The only memories we shall remember,
Is that of sticky blood lying upon clumped-up sand.

Of a dune,
in a faraway land,

For the suited ones have chained death,
To suns made of evil tome,
And in an effort to beckon holy light.

Did the evil ones finally find their home,
Bathed in unholy plight.

So, cry not little child,
Fear not danger,
Nor shadows in the wilds.

Death shall come peacefully,
And with a smile.

For in his bony skeletal heart,

Does he love the man,

The woman,

As well as the child.

For all are equal before his eyes,
And though the suited ones rule for a time.

The dead shall triumph once more,
Over the arrogant wise.

And until the day of reckoning comes,
Close your curtains,
And stay in your homes.

For death is at the beck and call of evil suits,
Whom with nary a man's eyes,
Can even bear the thought of holy fruit.

Death shall come once more,
Not as an evil god,
But as a friend forevermore.

To laugh in delight,
To share stories under the stars,
In a camp illuminated by firelight.

And one day will we laugh,

Together,

Under the stars,

As lovers shall embrace near and far,

For finally there'll be an end to war.

But until then, hide,

Stay under your bed and hide,

Because in the company of evil,

Do the suited ones puppeteer death,

And in misery and war,
Do they intend to confide.

The beautiful eyes of a lady fair

I gaze into the eyes of,
  A beautiful lady fair,

My eyes searching the depth and breadth of her wonder,
  Never tiring in my search,

For what do I search?
  I hardly know.
  An explorer am I.

And to this end do I search,
  In every nook and cranny of her eyes,
  Perhaps for the secrets of the universe.

Or perhaps a new line to add to rotting
  -Human verse.
  Perhaps another reason for wondrous rhyme.

But once more I gaze,
  With love in my heart, I gaze,
  My eyes transfixed.

Almost trance-like into her eyes.
  And so too,
  Was I too stupid to see.

That in the same breath,
  Was she gazing back at me.

Searching my eyes too,
  For something.
  Searching, my heart and core.

Possibly for something void of wrong,
  Perhaps for something worth this immense love.

So, we lay in each other's arms and search,
  Perhaps for the reason to our unfounded mirth.

When we see one another once more,

As the sight of the other shakes us to our core.

Once more we search,

Unable to look away,
  We search.

An eternity,

In each other's arms.

For a semblance of reason to our happiness.

For a simple explanation,

Of our silly mirth.

Perhaps it's a fool's game we play,
Searching for the reasons to love,

After we already,
Our hearts to one another,
Have dared to parlay.

Yet still we gaze,
Only this time with a kiss.

As we realise this.

Love is a fool's game anyway,

And we might as well play blindfolded.

Lest in one another's eyes
-We lose our way.

But a silly lovestruck man hardly takes advice,
From those who are much older and more wise.

So, gaze once more, I shall,
Forevermore into my doe-eyed beauty's soul, I shall.

For love is a strange thing,
A strange feeling, so to speak.

And perhaps I should learn of its power once more.

As my resolve is strewn across the floor.

And once more I say,

I will never cease to search,
   For what?
   I may never be sure.

But it's in my lover's eyes,
   The windows to her beautiful soul,

And that's all I really need to know.

Suits and shadows

What is at the end of an eternal path?
But for the scenery to test the souls of the walkers?
To test those of soft heart?

The way is rough and winding,
And never near a brook nor upon a rock to sit,
The sordid sun found ever more blinding.

As this path, we trod,
Wishing for an unholy place to lay our heads,
As we walk over shattered helmets and broken treads.

A desolate desert of man,
Metal and beast,
And creatures who in the night wail in want of feast.

And still, we walk,
Though the choking winter is over,
And evil ones, our souls do stalk.

We walk,

Where to?
  I guess we'll never know.

Except for the compass which never shows north,
  And the map which always changes course,
  We follow as we wander to and fro.

Man and woman,
  Hand in hand,
  Tow in tow.

A small innocent couple of humanity,
  Who wished from the suited ones' whip,
  To finally be free,

For an end to sordid sorrow.

So we walk,
  And wail,
  And talk.

As my lover and I remember the stories of beautiful lands of plenty,
  Duny sands of old,
  And the wondrous lack of woe.

They say that love was rampant,
  And the view of green grass and natural life
  -Never felt stagnant.

Not deserty sand or hopeless wail,

But even those who would take care of
-the saddened and the frail.

Such a world do I imagine with sigh,
As my lover's hand do I take,
As the children wince and wail and cry.

Onward we trod,
Searching for anything but desert,

Hoping for anything but fog.

Filled with strife.

And evil stalking beings,
Who hope to take your life.

In a terrible screech which will add to your lot.
Will they, their cufflinks caress,
As they call for their seething plot.

Oh, do not misunderstand,

I fear not the beings in this desert,
Though grotesque, ungodly and strange are they,
They are not clad in a suit.

So, to the monsters am truly I unafraid.

Not as fearful as,
The sun's we wished to tame

-The ones craving to acquire new lands.

I fear them more than the others,
The ones who plague the night,
With torches and firelight.

As they strike fear in the weak,
With frightening, seething evil,
As they willfully defile the meek.

They take as they please,
And relegate those who wish not to cause pain,
To the floor with a cry, as they strike their knees.

And their blood on the floor doth leave stain.
As they chokingly cry out in pain.

They hate and destroy the shadows,
The beings beyond life,
The beings who are said to inflict pain.

They fight and wreathe,

For though they also love life,
They cannot see a world,
Void of love and filled with strife.

So, we walk forevermore,
As pure, dark-clad evil follows suit,
With hands covered in moss, wearing a neatly ironed suit.

Riding a dangerous beast,
  Who with fire,
  Our flesh shall make into its feast.

We run,

We beg and we plea,

That the evils of this world,
  Would have mercy on our sordid melancholy.

That the shadows will lend some aid,
  That for once in my life,
  I won't feel mortally afraid.

Of creatures who scuttle underneath the city at night,
  Drinking the blood of the innocent as they fill the pious,
  with terrible, unholy fright,

While praying to the signs of hooded glee,
  As they hope,
  Joyous praise from the masses to bereave.

True evil haunts this desert,
  And it's not beast,
  It's not a monster who wills to make us into his feast.

For to this evil,
  Do even the devils run and wail,
  And so too, do the skeletons run and screech

This evil, clad in suit,

Rid of soul,

Kills your loved ones with a smile,

Keeping you alive as you choke on your blood,

As they take pleasure in your gasping wails,

And once more they will smile,
As they, your soul shall defile.

With hooded incantation and a sacrifice,

And in chains will they destroy the love of your life.
Relegating them to ashes,
Right before your terror-filled eyes.

The suited ones born of misery and strife.

And finally, when they've taken everything from you,

They won't even take your life,
Because to do so,
Would render you unable to feel more strife.

To do so, would be a waste of a wonderful, sordid view.

And with a smile, they'll take your hand,

Caressing it with musty breath,

And loving your misery.

Loving your sadness,

Leaving your soul broken and sore.

Gleaning joy from your tears,
As they intricately, their evil runes,
Upon your heart do score.

And once more they shall procure,
A neat suit for you to wear,
And in an incantation of old, sell your soul to the shadows of were.

Forevermore you shall now live,
To search the desert for weak, running ones,
And now in their gurgled misery find your joyous fun.

As you are one of them now,
For everything you've ever loved
-Was lost,

And the suited ones had finally won.

The thin white veil

Boney rickety claws,
Scratch hopelessly,
At the satin veil.

Between that which is known,
And that which is miserable and obscene,
As well as hidden and unseen.

The cracks of bones sewn together with tendon exposed,
And eye's still rotting,
Filling musty sockets,

As their will against the thin veil is imposed,
With hoarse screech, they scratch and tear,
Against the veil wielded by a beautiful lady fair.

Who gracefully winces at their sight,
Who in a soft tone,
Begs for them to find their eternal light.

"Go home dead ones,

There's naught but pain for you in the lands of the living"
Says she, as the names of the sordid ones.

In the Book of Death is written.

"Begone, let go,
I beg of thee.

Leave the land of the living,
Lest you all shan't ever be free"
She implores beyond the white veil in soft plea.

The dead ones hearken not,
Not for hopes of an evil plot,
But because they had forgotten their lot.

And still, they tear and scratch and seethe,

As the lady fair,
Hopes and begs and pleads.

For them to return to the lands of the dead,

To no longer be filled with sordid dread.

For they had forgotten the land of the free,
Was already the land of the dead.

And this too did the beings not perceive,
That the living would no longer recognise them.

And true life for them would only come,
  When they would turn away,
  To wander the land of peace.

When they return to the land of sadness,
  Void of pain and void of the ones,

Who in hopeless desperation,
  The masses had failed.

To return to the land beyond the white veil,

Across that eternal river to finally sail.

And once more death will prevail,
  With her beautiful eyes,
  And gentle white veil.

As she shall say to the dead,
  "Return my friends,

For the end,

Is your only choice,

Death is the only path,

Which is to your avail."

Melancholic art

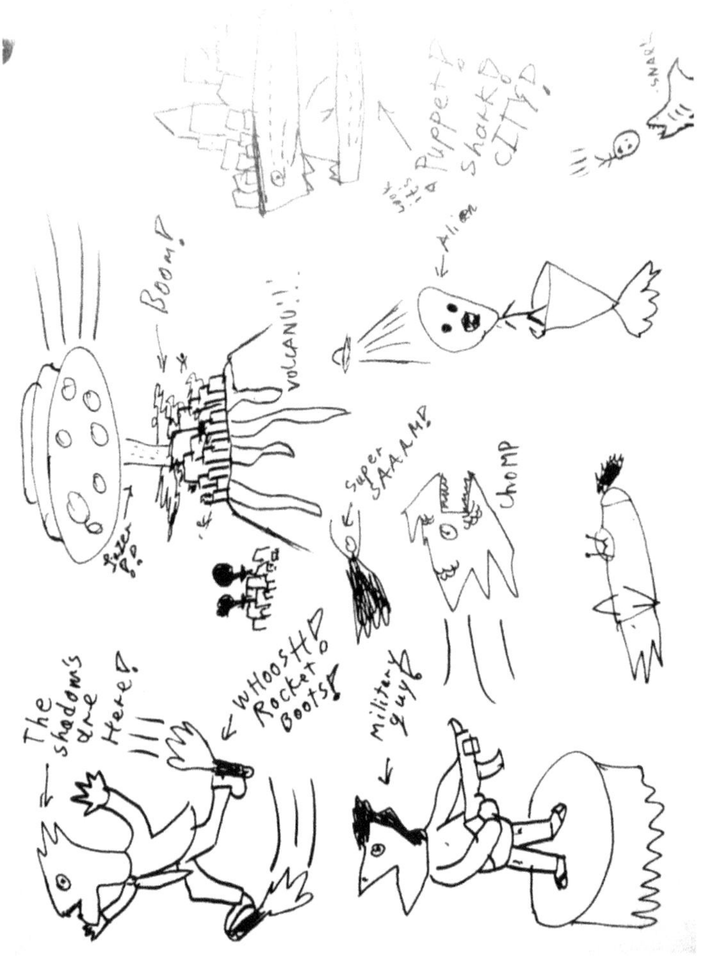
The shadows are Here!
WHOOSH! Rocket Boots!
Military guy!
Super SAAAM!
CHOMP
Boom!
Alien
Puppet! Shark! City!

sword
Explosion,
BOOM!
Boom
circle
The
Suited
ones never
lie!
Heya!

A short exploration of the philosophy of this book.

This book was an exploration of the darkness of the mind. Mind you, this isn't some sonnet on how one should live their life, as a matter of fact. Except for the poems on romance, I would implore everyone who reads this book to see the stories here as cautionary tales.

Or at least fairy tales, if I may be so bold as to elude at all, that my poetry exudes fairy tale polish. What I believe as a poet is that the world is composed of both choice and essence. In this way, I suppose my poetry is a desperate cry to create more from a normal life.

To leave something behind, so to speak. To this end, though it may be a challenging prospect, I believe that if nothing else. I can leave behind myself, composed in silly prose, on a stark white page.

I am one of many on this earth, you too are a human, are you not? Many of us are searching. For what? We may never know. And to some extent, this is okay. Why beg for the living to see the dead? When they wouldn't recognize them anyway?

My apologies, my philosophy is not the grandest, most entertaining nor most sincere. It is rooted in a state of acceptance and denial. And in the spirit of nihilism, is not the dichotomy of any state the purest form of horror? I suppose you can view every poem from the lens of your own experiences too. Yet, as was said, I implore everyone who has reached this point of the book. Please understand, that these are mostly cautionary tales.

Except for the tales of love. Excuse my romanticism, however, it was an important aspect of the writing of this book. It's the purest form of emotion I would say. A facet of horror itself.

And I love it because of this, romance the ultimate horror. To gaze deeper into the eyes of one you may love, and see the universe. Quite profound, and something I can never hope to understand.

Don't mind me, fair reader, I am but a man of allegory and thought. You may have noticed that there is no clear philosophy spoken of here, and I suppose that is true. All I can say is that I thank you for purchasing and reading this book. Of course, unless you pirated it, but even then, thank you. For letting this silly poet spend a while with you.

In conversation with a close friend through rhyme and prose. I suppose it may be a strange thing for a poet to say. But yet again, I thank you for letting me spend some time sharing my universe of thought, exploration, wonder, terror, gnashing of teeth and pure love.

And I hope that you can see that, in exploration of the worlds of terror I concocted out of my silly mind. That you can find the beautiful world outside more, wondrous, beautiful and sublime, in comparison.

Oh, but do make sure to follow my warnings, dear reader. There's a thin veil between life and death, and don't mind the eyes staring back at you.

...

I jest, I suppose.

And once more dear reader, look for life, look for love and never give in. The future is wrung of the trust and hope we may have in the present. You will always find solace in the arms of a lover and there is naught but love that can change a heart.

Yes, I know, pragmatism and fact and truth. They coerce us into nihilism. But I say no! Never to follow the will of others! But my own!

And this fact I will always relish, that I am the captain of my ship, and I will always be the one who chooses my own melancholy. Existentialism may be the philosophy here then. Or perhaps it's pessimism. But mostly, it's an acknowledgement of nothing and everything.

And how this universe is more than chaotic, it's more than

order. It's something else...

Sinister perhaps? Maybe not. Perhaps it's the embodiment of feminine beauty. Perhaps we are all just jesters dancing a Waltz of eternal thought. Moving from ballroom floor to ballroom floor as we gaze into the eyes of a wonderful lover.

My apologies, I tend to ramble on don't I? I won't take much more of your time. I simply wanted to say thank you and someday we will see the future. Full of love and pain, and every part of it will be built by us. Our hopes and dreams, and yes, perhaps a few of our ghostly charms.

So finally, I will end this book with a metaphorical tip of the hat, a slight jester's bow and the farewell of a dear friend.

Until next time...

Take care.

-Mike H. Ale

Before you go!

I have started a simple Gmail account for any questions, thoughts, ideas or general mail that you'd like to send! Don't hesitate to reach out and I'll do my best to answer any mail that comes through.

- **mikehale.jsm@gmail.com**

www.ingramcontent.com/pod-product-compliance
Lightning Source LLC
LaVergne TN
LVHW010607100826
845148LV00014B/2879

* 9 7 8 0 7 9 6 1 3 9 9 8 6 *